T0222572

Beginning Unity Android Game Development

From Beginner to Pro

Kishan Takoordyal

Apress®

Beginning Unity Android Game Development: From Beginner to Pro

Kishan Takoordyal
Eau Coulee, Mauritius

ISBN-13 (pbk): 978-1-4842-6001-2   ISBN-13 (electronic): 978-1-4842-6002-9
https://doi.org/10.1007/978-1-4842-6002-9

Managing Director, Apress Media LLC: Welmoed Spahr
Acquisitions Editor: Spandana Chatterjee
Development Editor: Matthew Moodie
Coordinating Editor: Divya Modi

Cover designed by eStudioCalamar

Cover image designed by Pixabay

Distributed to the book trade worldwide by Springer Science+Business Media New York, 233 Spring Street, 6th Floor, New York, NY 10013. Phone 1-800-SPRINGER, fax (201) 348-4505, e-mail orders-ny@springer-sbm.com, or visit www.springeronline.com. Apress Media, LLC is a California LLC and the sole member (owner) is Springer Science+Business Media Finance Inc (SSBM Finance Inc). SSBM Finance Inc is a Delaware corporation.

For information on translations, please e-mail rights@apress.com, or visit www.apress.com/rights-permissions.

Apress titles may be purchased in bulk for academic, corporate, or promotional use. eBook versions and licenses are also available for most titles. For more information, reference our Print and eBook Bulk Sales web page at www.apress.com/bulk-sales.

Any source code or other supplementary material referenced by the author in this book is available to readers on GitHub via the book's product page, located at www.apress.com/978-1-4842-6001-2. For more detailed information, please visit www.apress.com/source-code.

Printed on acid-free paper

To my family and the high school friends who have supported me from the start

Table of Contents

About the Author

Kishan Takoordyal started at a young age by learning programming with Python. Since acquiring a greater interest in game development, he has been developing games, using the Unity game engine for more than four years. He is also a Linux aficionado and has worked on his own distribution. Currently, he resides in his home country, Mauritius, where he often participates in major technical events and hackathons with Cyberstorm.mu, while developing quality games and improving his portfolio with new skills.

About the Technical Reviewer

 **Simon Jackson** is a longtime software engineer and architect with many years of Unity game development experience, as well as the author of several Unity game development books. He loves to create Unity projects as well as lend a hand to help educate others, whether via a blog, vlog, user group, or major speaking event.

His primary focus at the moment is the XRTK (Mixed Reality Toolkit) project. This is aimed at building a cross-platform mixed reality framework to enable both VR and AR developers to build efficient solutions in Unity and then build/ distribute them to as many platforms as possible.

Introduction

This book aims to help readers master the art of programming game apps for Android, using the Unity3D game engine. It will help those wishing to pursue a career, or hobbyists, understand basic concepts of game development, using Unity. By the end of the book, readers will have gained sufficient knowledge to confidently build an Android game.

The book starts by explaining simple programming concepts, to familiarize beginners with the relevant jargon. Readers will then learn to navigate the Unity interface and use basic tools (`hand`, `move`, `rotate`, `scale`, `rect`). They will also learn to create basic 3D objects in the game, while getting to know the purpose of several windows (Hierarchy, Inspector, Scene, Game, Console, Project, Asset Store). The role of prefabs, Canvas UI elements (such as `Text`, `Button`, `Image`, etc.), and several components (`transform`, `renderer`, `collider`, `rigidbody`, etc.) will also be discussed.

In the last chapters, readers will learn to create a simple game for Android, using the concepts studied in the previous chapters. Scripts will have to be written to handle the behaviors of the player and enemies, as well to handle other aspects of the game.

A lot of `MonoBehavior` structs (`Vector3`, `Quaternion`) and functions (`Awake`, `Start`, `Update`, `FixedUpdate`, `OnCollisionEnter`, `Coroutine`) also will be explained. Tips, such as switching to the universal rendering pipeline, if targeting mobile platforms, will also be shared throughout the book, to help improve in-game performance.

By the end of the book, the reader will have gained solid knowledge for making basic Android games that can be upgraded later to make more complex versions.

CHAPTER 1

Programming Concepts

Programming is all about taking a problem and defining a solution for it. Every detail is elaborated to try and convey that solution to a computer. For some, specific instructions are given to the computer system, to perform tasks leading to the desired solution.

Thankfully, there are high-level programming languages to help us write these solutions in a language closer to English than to 0s and 1s. In exact terms, a programming language is a set of rules that provides a means of instructing a computer what operations to perform.

Let's consider an analogy. (Refer to Figure 1-1.) Suppose that we have a couple of fruits and must make a salad out of them. The first step is to analyze and define the problem. Specifically, input data (fruits) must be identified and turned into expected output data (salad).

The second step is planning. One technique that programmers make use of are flowcharts, which are a pictorial representation of a step-by-step solution to a problem. They help us to focus on the program logic rather than on the appropriate syntax of the programming language we'll use.

© Kishan Takoordyal 2020
K. Takoordyal, *Beginning Unity Android Game Development*,
https://doi.org/10.1007/978-1-4842-6002-9_1

The third step consists of actually coding the program. The logic in the second step must now be converted into something that the computer can understand. Various integrated development environments (IDEs) exist to help programmers code in the programming language of their choice. An IDE is just like a text editor but has several additional features to help the development of a program, such as auto-completion or a debugger. Auto-completion is a feature whereby sentences are automatically completed with keywords that the IDE expects next, while a debugger helps to run the program and possibly find bugs.

The fourth and final step is to test the program. A few errors might be present, and to detect them, different types of test data must be input, and the output must be consistent with the expected result. Debugging refers to detecting, locating, and correcting bugs. These bugs might be syntax or logical ones, among others, the former being, for example, a misspelled instruction that the computer doesn't understand, and the latter being something like telling the computer to repeat an operation but not telling it how to stop repeating.

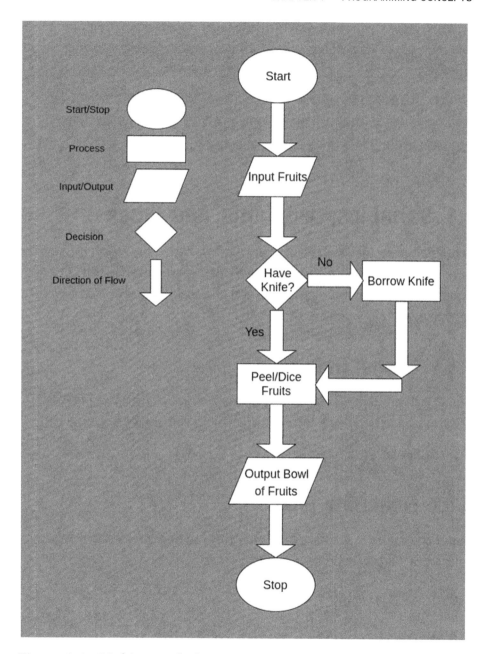

Figure 1-1. *Making a salad*

This chapter will guide you through many popular programming concepts, but to keep things simple, a lot of content will be set aside.

Note   You won't be able to run the following code snippets yet, but don't worry. They are meant only to give you some basic theory before we jump into Unity coding in subsequent chapters.

1.1 Variables, Constants, and Types

In programming, data can be of many different types. As we will be working with the Unity game engine, snippets (parts) of code will be expressed in C#. For this chapter, we will be considering only four types of data: integer, float, boolean, and string.

1.1.1 Integer Data Type

Numerical values that are whole numbers (without a fractional part) can be expressed in an integer form. Integer values can also be negative.

```
10, 2667, -50, 0
```

1.1.2 Float Data Type

Numerical values that have a fractional part can be expressed in a floating-point form. Float values can also be negative.

```
3.9874, 1.245, -112.245, 0.0932
```

1.1.3 Boolean Data Type

Boolean values have a value either of true or false.

1.1.4 String Data Type

Sets of characters can be expressed in string form.

```
"Unity", "192.168.100.0", "The big brown fox"
```

1.1.5 Variables

Different operations can be performed on all sorts of data. In the long run, it might be a good idea to make use of variables. A variable is a type of special container to hold a specific kind of data. As an analogy, a variable may be a wardrobe that serves to hold clothes and nothing else—not kitchen utensils, for example. In C#, the classic way of declaring a variable is as follows:

```
<variableType> <variableName> = <value>;
```

In C#, a variable of a particular data type *cannot* hold values of another data type. To be clear, to declare and assign values to variables of the data types mentioned, something similar to the following would have to be set up:

```
int myInteger = 10;
float myFloat = 3.9874f;
bool myBool = false;
string myString = "Unity";
```

Note that for floating-point variables, f must be appended at the end of the float value, to make sure that it is interpreted as a float (rather than the double data type). In the double data type, values are stored in 64 bits (maximum 16 digits), which is not so useful for the type of values we will be dealing with. Using a float data type also provides more performance overall, because data is stored in 32 bits (7 digits).

If variables are initialized without a value, for example, `bool` `condition`, the default value of the data type they're using will be assigned to them, in the case of this example, `false`. For integers and floats, the default values will be equal to `0` and `0.0f`, respectively. For strings, this will be `""` (a blank and empty string).

If a variable already contains a value, and a new value is assigned to it, the contents of the variable will be overwritten, and it will contain the newly assigned value until the end of the program, unless another value is assigned to it.

```
int pin = 1234;
pin = 4321;
// pin now holds a value of 4321.
```

Note that if a variable has already been declared, there's no need to reference it with its data type. This will be discussed more thoroughly in Section 1.7.

1.1.6 Constants

Constants are just like variables, except that they can't be modified after declaration and will keep the value they were initialized with. The process to declare a constant is similar to that to declare variables, except that the `const` keyword must be placed before the data type field.

```
const <variableType> <variableName> = <value>;
```

1.1.7 Comments

A comment is a programmer-readable annotation or explanation in a script that usually makes it easier for users to understand what some part of a code does. Comments are generally ignored by the compiler/ interpreter. In C#, comments can be written either in a single-line or multiline way.

```
// This is a single-line comment.
/* This is a multiline comment.*/
```

1.2 Arrays

An array is a form of data storage structure similar to a variable, in the sense that it is declared to hold a specific data type. Unlike variables, however, arrays can hold multiple data values. When an array is created, a predefined size is set for it. The array will thus hold the number of data values equal to its size.

Data values found at indexes (positions) in the array may, just like variables, be read, modified, or replaced by other data values of the same type. The index of an array starts at 0 (the first data value), and the last index will be equal to the size of the array minus one, because the first index isn't one.

1.2.1 Declaring and Creating an Array

If an array is declared without the part after the equal sign, it will just have a size of zero. The size of the array can be modified later, but data values stored at each index will be reset to the default value of the data type the array uses.

```
<arrayType>[] <arrayName> = new <arrayType>[<size>];

// create an integer array of a size of 5 named firstArray
int[] firstArray = new int[5];
// create a string array with a size of 0 named secondArray
string[] secondArray;
```

```
// creating a new string array with a size of 10 and assigning
it to secondArray
secondArray = new string[10];
```

Another way of declaring arrays could be to initialize them with values at the start.

```
<arrayType>[] <arrayName> = {<value0>, <value1>};
```

```
int[] firstArray = {5, 10, 20, 35, 45};
string[] secondArray;
```

```
secondArray = {"abc", "def", "ghi"};
```

To get the length of an array, that is, how many values it can store, the Length method can be called.

```
int[] firstArray = {5, 10, 20, 35, 45};
int arraySize = firstArray.Length; // 5
```

1.2.2 Setting, Fetching, and Modifying Values in an Array

In this section, we are going to look at how to set and modify values at indexes in an array.

```
<arrayName>[<index>] = <value>;
<variable> = <arrayName>[<index>];
```

In the following example, the value 13 will be stored in the third position (index 2) of the integer array being used (firstArray). The value 13 is obtained by adding the data values being stored at index 0 (7) and index 4 (6) where size - 1 refers to index 4.

```
int[] firstArray;
int size = 5;

firstArray = new int[size];
firstArray[0] = 7;
firstArray[4] = 6;

firstArray[2] = firstArray[0] + firstArray[size - 1];
```

1.3 Arithmetic Operators

It is common to perform arithmetic operations in programming. The basic arithmetic operations are addition, subtraction, multiplication, and division. Numerical values can be manipulated using these operators. This also applies to variables and constants that hold numerical values (int, float). Arithmetic operators must have two operands, and multiples of them can be chained for one equation. An operand is anything that is used with an operator. For example, numbers in an addition statement are operands, and the plus sign is an operator. An order of operations is respected: operations in parentheses are evaluated first, followed by those for division and multiplication and, finally, addition and subtraction.

1.3.1 Addition, Subtraction, Multiplication, and Division

These can be used just as you learned in math class.

```
1 + 1; // 2
9 -6; // 3
4 * 2; // 8
60 / 12; // 5
6 * 2 + 3; // 15
5 * (3 - 1) + 1; // 11
```

1.3.2 Variables and Constants

As previously stated, arithmetic operations can be done by using variables or constants that hold numerical values.

```
int number = 1;

number + 1; // 2
number + 8 - 6; // 3
```

Results of arithmetic operations can also be stored in variables of a numerical type.

```
int number = 2;

number = number * 2; // 4
number * 4; // 16

number = number + 56; // 60
number / 12; // 5
```

1.3.3 Modulus

This is another useful arithmetic operator. It returns the remainder of an integer division. Just as in the preceding operators, it can also be used with variables and constants.

```
11 % 4; // 3
```

1.3.4 Compound Assignment Operators

There's a shorthand way of assigning the value of an operation to a variable that is involved in that operation.

Example	Equivalent
sheep += 5;	sheep = sheep + 5;
sheep -= 5;	sheep = sheep - 5;
sheep *-= 5;	sheep = sheep * 5;
sheep /= 5;	sheep = sheep / 5;
sheep %= 5;	sheep = sheep % 5;

1.3.5 Quick Increment and Decrement

Variables can be incremented or decremented by 1 rapidly.

```
int count = 5;

count++; // 6
count++; // 7
count--; // 6
```

1.3.6 Unary Operations

A unary operation is an operation with only one operand. As unary operations have only one operand, they are evaluated before other operations containing them. This usually applies to positive and negative operators. For example, +8 + -2 and +2 - -3 are the equivalents of 8 - 2 and 2 + 5, respectively.

1.3.7 Casting

It may happen that when performing arithmetic operations, for instance, an output of the undesired type is obtained. For example, if a programmer has a variable declared as an integer in which they are about to store the result of 5 * 1.61f, a float result will be obtained that can't be stored in that variable.

This is one of the situations in which casting comes in. Basically, casting transforms a value of a particular data type into the same value, but of a specified data type. Casting a float to an integer doesn't round the value. Only the integer part is returned.

```
int perfectInt;
float badFloat;

badFloat = 5 * 1.61f; // 7.55f

perfectInt = (int)badFloat; // 7
```

In the preceding example, we cast the value of the variable badFloat to perfectInt. We could, however, have directly performed the arithmetic operation and cast it in an integer in the perfectInt variable directly. For arithmetic operations where a float result is expected, there is no need to cast integers involved (whether in a variable or a raw value) to a float data type

Casting may also be inapplicable in some cases. For example, a stringvalue comprised of letters can't be cast to an integer or float.

1.4 Logical Operators

Logical operators in C# are symbols that are used to connect expressions, such that the value of the compound expression produced depends on that of the original expressions and on the meaning of the logical operator(s) used.

1.4.1 Simple Boolean Expressions

Boolean expressions always result in either a `true` or `false`. For example, asking a question such as Is 5 greater than 2? would result in yes. In programming, this would be written as 5 > 2, and the resulting Boolean value returned would be `true`.

Symbol	Interpretation
==	Is equal to
!=	Is not equal to
>	Is greater than
<	Is less than
>=	Is greater or equal to
<=	Is less than or equal to

```
4 > 5 // false
180 < 450 // true
60 >= 70 // false
567 <= 550 // false
330 != 80 // true

45 > 45 // false
40 < 40.1f // true
90 >= 90 // true
1 == 2 // false

"Cat" == "Dog" // false
"cat" == "Cat" // false
"Shoes" == "Shoes" // true
"Car" != "Plane" // true
```

1.4.2 AND (&&)

The AND logical operator takes two operands. It returns a value of true if the operands result in true.

```
(1 == 1) && (5 > 4) // true
(3 > 4) && (80 >= 79) && (50 > 40) // false
```

1.4.3 OR (||)

The OR logical operator takes two operands. It returns a value of true if at least one of its operands results in true.

```
(3 < 4) || ( 255 == 256) // true
(4 > 5) || (40 < 50) || ("abc" == "def") // false
```

1.4.4 NOT (!)

The NOT logical operator takes only one operand. It turns a Boolean value into its counterpart. That is, if the Boolean value of its operand is true, it will return false.

```
!(1 == 2) // true
!((4 <= 8) && (6.1 >= 6)) // false
```

1.5 Selection

Normally, scripts are comprised of many lines of code. The sequence of instructions is performed one after another. Sometimes, we wish to run particular instructions based on specific conditions only. That's where selection comes in. By asking some sort of question, we can have the computer system do something based on the answer. Control structures are what help us change this flow in programming. Every control structure requires the indentation of code placed inside it. Indentation is really just spaces or tabs.

1.5.1 if then else Control Structure

In this selection control structure, the condition of all the clauses specified will be checked in the normal flow the code is running until the first condition that results in true is found, or if all of them result in false. If the condition of a clause results in true, its code block will run, and all the other clauses will be skipped, because only one of the clauses specified can be run.

Using a very simple if then else, some code can be performed only if the specified condition results in true.

```
if (condition) {
 // Do something
}
string apple = "fruit";
int numberOfFruits = 0;

if (apple == "fruit") {
 numberOfFruits++;
}
```

The else keyword can also be specified to make another block of code run, if the condition in the if clause results in false instead.

```
if (condition) {
 // Do something
} else {
 // Do something else instead
}
```

```
string apple = "fruit";
int numberOfFruits = 0;
int numberOfVegetables = 0;

if (apple == "fruit") {
 numberOfFruits++;
} else {
 numberOfVegetables++;
}
```

Additionally, if and else clauses can be used together to make multiple conditions in one block only. Note that the last else clause can be omitted.

```
if (condition) {
 // Do something
} else if (another condition) {
 // Do something
} else {
 // Do something else instead
}

string gender = "M";
int males = 0;
int females = 0;
int undefined = 0;

if (gender == "M") {
 males++;
} else if (gender == "F") {
 females++;
} else {
 undefined++;
}
```

Finally, if then else control structures can be "nested" into other if then else control structures.

```
if (condition) {
 if (condition) {
 // Do something
 }
}

string species = "human";
string furColor = "";
int brownFur = 0;
int blackFur = 0;

// != is interpreted as "is not equal to"
if (species != "human") {
 if (furColor == "brown") {
 brownFur++;
 } else if (furColor == "black") {
 blackFur++;
 }
}
```

1.5.2 Case Control Structure

A case selection control structure works with a variable, and depending on the value it contains, specific code can be run. All the case clauses will be verified until one of them has a condition that results in true; otherwise, the code in the last clause, default, will be run. If one of the case clauses has a condition that results in true, the respective code block will be run, and all the remaining clauses won't be verified and, thus, skipped. The break keyword is required in each clause. This form of control structure is useful in the event that many checks have to be performed, as it provides a more elegant solution than chaining many if-else statements.

```
switch(variable) {
 case value:
 // Do something
 break;
 default:
 // Do something else then
 break;
}

string apple = "fruit";
int numberOfFruits = 0;
int numberOfVegetables = 0;
int numberOfExceptions = 0;

switch (apple) {
 case "fruit":
 numberOfFruits++;
 break;
 case "vegetable":
 numberOfVegetables++;
 break;
 default:
 numberOfExceptions++;
 break;
}
```

1.6 Iteration

Very often, some parts of a script may have to be repeated more than once. Instead of duplicating the code x times, to keep the program easier to read, modify, and debug, and, in some cases, make algorithms significantly more efficient, loop control structures may be used. Code placed between the curly braces of loop control structure clauses will keep running, based on a predefined condition. If, however, a condition always remains `true`, the loop will run infinitely and cause the program to crash.

1.6.1 while Loop

Essentially, code in a `while` loop keeps on repeating itself while some condition is `true`.

```
while (condition) {
 // Do something
}
```

In the following example, the `while` loop runs five times.

```
int number = 1;

while (number < 6) {
 number++;
}
```

1.6.2 for Loop

A `for` loop is a bit more complex to write than a `while` loop. Unlike the latter, it doesn't have just a condition. Rather, it involves declaring a variable, setting a condition, which, if doesn't result in true, causes the loop to stop running, and, finally, setting the amount by which the variable will be incremented/decremented each time.

```
for (<declareVariable>; <condition>; <variableIncrement>)
{
 // Do something
}
```

For example, a for loop can be used to perform the sum of all the even numbers from 2 to 10. Basically, a variable, i, is declared as an integer, initially given the value 2, and each time the loops run, its value will be incremented by 2 and added to the variable sum, until i has a value greater than 10.

```
int evenSum = 0;

for (int i = 2; i <= 10; i += 2) {
 evenSum += i;
}
```

1.6.3 foreach Loop

This is a slightly modified version of the for loop and is more common to use with structures such as arrays. Instead of writing a for loop to loop through all values of an array, a foreach loop can be written quicker, which gets the work done. Unlike the regular for loop, in which the size of the array has to be written for the condition part, that's not necessary for a foreach loop.

```
foreach (<dataType> <newVariableName> in <arrayName>) {
 // Do something
}
```

For example, let's imagine that we have an array of float values and wish to get the sum of all the elements of that array. The foreach loop will loop through every element of the array values and, each time, automatically assign the current element to the temporary float variable temp, which will itself be added and stored in the variable sum.

```
float[] values = {66.3f, 346.21f, 45.8f, 890.8f, 556.99f};
float sum = 0.0f;
```

```
foreach (float temp in values) {
 sum += temp;
}
```

For reference, here's the equivalent in a normal for loop. Note that values.Length returns a value of 5, but the loop cannot be equal to this, because the last index of the array will be 4.

```
float[] values = {66.3f, 346.21f, 45.8f, 890.8f, 556.99f};
float sum = 0.0f;

for (int i = 0; i < values.Length; i++) {
 float temp = values[i];
 sum += temp;
}
```

1.6.4 Continue and Break

The continue keyword "tells" a loop to skip any code remaining and directly jump to the next iteration of the loop. A simple example could be iterating through an array of food and simply jumping to the next instance of the iteration, to avoid incrementing an integer variable if the element of the array at the current position isn't a fruit.

```
string[] food = {"fruit", "human", "fruit", "vegetable", "shoes"};
int fruits;

foreach (string current in food) {
 if (current != "fruit") {
 continue;
 }
 fruits++;
}
```

The break keyword instantly ends the execution of a loop and jumps to the line of code just after and outside the loop. It can be used to end the execution of a loop once a particular value has been found in an array, for example, because it's futile to continue checking the rest of the elements of that array.

```
string[] alphabets = {"a", "b", "c", "d", "e", "f"};
string alphabetToSearchFor = "c";

int alphabetRealPosition = 0;

for (int i = 0; i < alphabets.Length; i++) {
 if (alphabets[i] == alphabetToSearchFor) {
 alphabetRealPosition = i + 1;
 break;
 }
}
```

1.7 Functions

You could have scripts with hundreds or thousands of lines of code. While you can write everything in one continuous flow, wrapping code doing one specific thing in one function makes the code appear more tidy, and it's easier to manage. In the preceding "Iteration" section (1.6), we learned how to decrease code duplication by making loops. But what if some code has to be run again multiple times but at different parts of the program? That's where functions come in.

1.7.1 Basics

Functions contain code, and at desired parts in the script, they can be "called" to perform the operation they were written to do.

```
void <functionName> () {
 // Do something
}
```

Note that functions that do not return any value, that is, the script doesn't expect a value from them, have the type void. A void function accomplishes its task and then returns control to the caller.

A simple function can be used to display something to the user. Of course, the function won't run by itself. That's why in the main flow that our code is running, we have to call it. The Debug.Log function will output a logging message of the string we pass to it.

```
PrintHelloWorld();

void PrintHelloWorld() {
 Debug.Log("Hello World");
}
```

1.7.2 Parameters

At times, we might also want to pass values to our functions, so that they perform an operation with those, if, for example, we wish to reuse that function for similar operations but with different values. The values that we pass to functions are known as *parameters*, and they must be of the same data type as the actual parameters.

```
void <functionName> (<parameterType> <parameterName>) {
 // Do something
}
```

Modifying the preceding example, we now want the function to print the sum of three numbers passed as parameters. The values passed are identified by a local name in the function, so that they can be referenced. The result of the sum is 11 and will be outputted in a logging message.

```
int a = 5;
int b = 4;

PrintSum(a, b, 2);

void PrintSum(int first, int second, int third) {
 Debug.Log(first + second + third);
}
```

1.7.3 Returning a Value

In the previous examples, our functions only performed an operation. They didn't in the true sense "return" a value. Functions not declared as void can return a value that can be assigned to variables or used to control the flow. For example, instead of making boolean variables to hold a boolean value being returned by a function to be used in an if else condition, we can directly call the function in the if clause. Note that when a function returns a value, that value must be preceded by the return keyword, and any code, if left in that function, won't run.

```
<functionType> <functionName> (<parameterType> <parameterName>)
{
 // Do something
 return <value>;
}
```

Taking the preceding example again, let's assign the return value of the function to c this time.

```
int a = 5;
```

```
int b = 4;
int c = 0;

c = Add3Numbers(a, b, 2);

int Add3Numbers(int first, int second, int third) {
 return first + second + third;
}
```

Let's consider another example, this time with a boolean value. The function will return false if the variable eat doesn't contain the value fruit.

```
string food = "fruit";
int numberFruits = 0;

if (itsAFruit(food)) {
 numberFruits++;
}

bool itsAFruit(string eat) {
 if (eat == "fruit") {
 return true;
 }
 return false;
}
```

1.7.4 global and local

Basically, variables declared outside all the functions of a script are known as global, while those declared inside of functions are known as local. global variables can be accessed from anywhere inside the script, while local variables can only be accessed inside the function they are declared in.

In the following example, a is a global variable, because it and its value can be accessed, read, and modified anywhere in the script. Even if a global variable is passed to a function as a parameter, the name by which that function has referenced the parameter being passed is known only to itself and, thus, both b and c are local parameters that can only be accessed, read, and modified inside the function temporaryFunction().

```
int a = 100;

void temporaryFunction(string b) {
  int c;
}
```

1.8 Coroutines

Coroutines are very similar to functions, except that when you call a function, it runs to completion before returning. Any action that takes place in a function isn't something that happens over time, as code in a function is run within a single frame update. While it is possible to use loops and checks to achieve this, it is often more useful to use a coroutine. Unlike functions, which must be manually called each time to be executed, coroutines can be set to run automatically at specified delays. Return values from a coroutine are compulsory and may not be assigned to any variable or used directly.

1.8.1 Defining and Calling Coroutines

A coroutine can be called only once, and code within it will be run at a number of frames defined by some specific keywords.

```
StartCoroutine("<coroutineName>"); // or
StartCoroutine(<coroutineName>());
IEnumerator <coroutineName>(<parameters>) {
 // Do something
 yield return <returnValue>;
}
```

A coroutine always is defined as IEnumerator and must always have that yield return <returnValue>; line. Any code after that yield return <returnValue>; line will be run after the amount of frames specified as the returnValue.

For example, to increase the value of the integer variable numberFrames by one each time a frame is run in a game, the following code may be used. yield return null; is the equivalent of yield return 1; which, in our case, causes the last line of the coroutine to be ran once per frame.

```
int numberFrames = 0;
StartCoroutine("CountFrames");
IEnumerator CountFrames() {
 yield return null;
 numberFrames++;
}
```

1.8.2 Using Seconds Instead of Frames

Instead of waiting for frames, coroutines can wait for a number of seconds.

```
IEnumerator <coroutineName>(<parameters>) {
 // Do something
 yield return new WaitForSeconds(<numberOfSeconds>);
}
```

A good example to demonstrate this could be checking for some conditions at particular time intervals, rather than at each frame. The `for` clause specified following runs infinitely. The `if` clause will run at intervals of the value passed as parameter.

```
string weather = "rainy";
bool happy = false;
float numberSeconds = 0.5f;
StartCoroutine(CheckWeather(numberSeconds));
IEnumerator CheckWeather(float amount) {
 for ( ; ; ) {
 yield return new WaitForSeconds(amount);
 if (weather == "sunny") {
 happy = true;
 } else {
 happy = false;
 }
 }
}
```

CHAPTER 2

Introduction to Unity

As you already know, we will be using the Unity game engine in order to develop games. Unity has been written in the C++ programming language, but its scripting application programming interface (API; what we'll use to actually code the games) is in C#. Unity can be used for much more than just making games. It can even be used to create visualizations for movies, architecture, or car manufacturing.

The benefit of using Unity rather than writing our games from scratch is that Unity already provides many ready-made tools to assist us in our game-making process, such as physics or lighting. Compared to other game engines, Unity is far more popular, which makes resolving bugs or learning how to do something easier, because it is very likely that something will already be present on the Internet. Any games we wish to work on in Unity is a project.

2.1 Creating a Unity Account

You must have an account set up at `https://id.unity.com` in order to use Unity. As well, you can create an account using your Google or Facebook account (Figure 2-1).

© Kishan Takoordyal 2020
K. Takoordyal, *Beginning Unity Android Game Development*,
https://doi.org/10.1007/978-1-4842-6002-9_2

Figure 2-1. *Creating a Unity account*

2.2 Downloading Unity and Add-ons

Unity has four licenses: Personal, Plus, Pro, and Enterprise. Personal
has most of the features offered in the other business licenses and is free
(Figure 2-2). Plus can be purchased by individuals who want more features
than Personal offers. Pro or Enterprise licenses must be purchased if
income derived from your game-developing business or organization
exceeds a particular threshold. The greatest advantages that you'll be
forfeiting by using a Personal license are the ability to customize the
splash screen of your game (when the game starts), the use of a dark
editor UI, greater support, availability of premium resources (although not
absolutely required), and more diagnostics/analytics. More information
can be found at `https://store.unity.com/`.

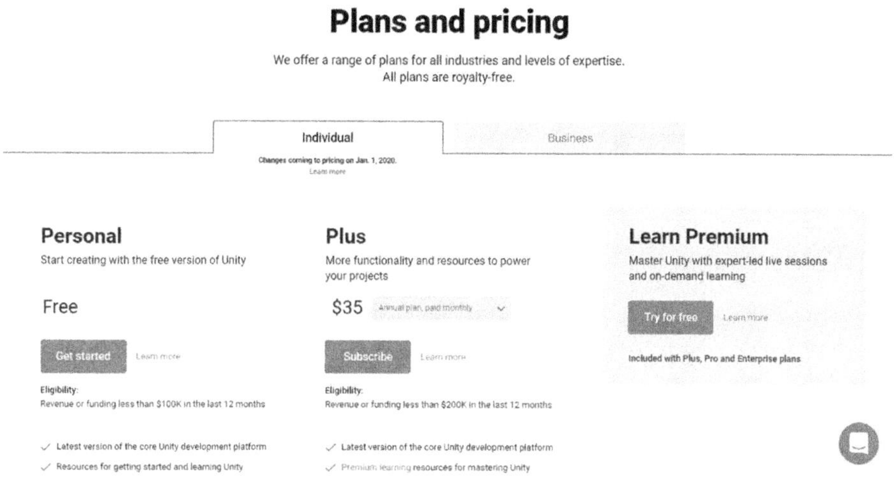

Plans and pricing

We offer a range of plans for all industries and levels of expertise.
All plans are royalty-free.

Individual	Business

Changes coming to pricing on Jan. 1, 2020.
Learn more

Personal

Start creating with the free version of Unity

Free

Get started   Learn more

Eligibility:
Revenue or funding less than $100K in the last 12 months

✓ Latest version of the core Unity development platform
✓ Resources for getting started and learning Unity

Plus

More functionality and resources to power
your projects

$35   Annual plan, paid monthly   ⌄

Subscribe   Learn more

Eligibility:
Revenue or funding less than $200K in the last 12 months

✓ Latest version of the core Unity development platform
✓ Premium learning resources for mastering Unity

Learn Premium

Master Unity with expert-led live sessions
and on-demand learning

Try for free   Learn more

Included with Plus, Pro and Enterprise plans

Figure 2-2. *Unity plans*

2.2.1 Unity Hub

Unity Hub is an application that can be used to download several versions
of Unity, along with their respective modules, if required, and contains
a list of the projects (cloud or local) you're working on or have created
(Figure 2-3).

Figure 2-3. *Unity Hub projects*

For MacOS or Windows users, Unity Hub can be downloaded from
`https://unity3d.com/get-unity/download/`, and for Linux users, an
executable file can be obtained from the forum at `https://forum.unity.`
`com/threads/unity-hub-v2-0-0-release.677485/`. Just install or run it
after it finishes downloading.

Next, you must download a version of the Unity Editor (the actual game
engine). You'll have to use any 2019.3.x version for the examples in this book.
Sign in to Unity Hub first, with the credentials you previously used to create
an account. Then, proceed to click your profile picture or initials (top-right
corner). Go to Manage License and activate a new Unity Personal license.
Finally, go to Installs, click Add, select a 2019.3.x version of Unity, and
choose the modules you wish to install. As we will be working on a mobile
game, choose at least Android and/or iOS Build Support modules. Note that
you will not be able to make iOS games if you don't have an Apple computer.
For Android build support, check Android SDK & NDK Tools and OpenJDK,
too (Figure 2-4). The documentation and everything else is optional.

Figure 2-4. *Downloading the Unity Editor from the Hub*

You will also require an integrated development environment (IDE) to write scripts. Visual Studio Code is a lightweight and excellent choice. You can download it from `https://code.visualstudio.com/`. We will be linking it to the Unity Editor later. For now, just install it.

2.2.2 Creating an Empty Project

In Unity Hub, click the blue New button, name the project you're about to create, and choose a location in which to store it. Choose 3D as the template. Click Create, wait a while, and the project should open (Figure 2-5).

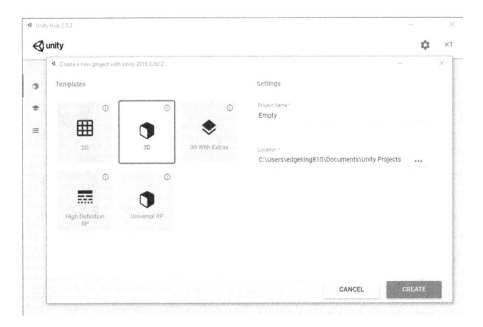

Figure 2-5. *Creating a new project*

First, go to Edit ➤ Preferences ➤ External Tools and make sure you're using the built-in JDK, SDK, and NDK. The appropriate check boxes should be ticked. You will also have to assign the vscode option in the External Script Editor tab, to write and modify scripts in a proper IDE. This option is just under the External Tools header (Figure 2-6).

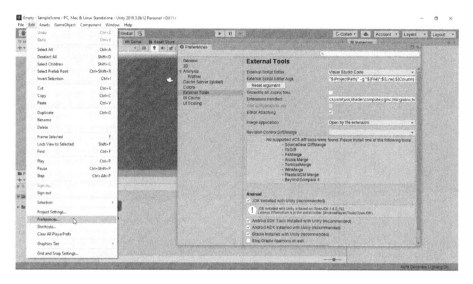

Figure 2-6. *Checking preferences*

2.3 Essential Windows

Unity provides several windows with very specific features to help developers in their game-developing process. You already know what a project means in Unity. Game projects contain scenes. Think of scenes as levels of a game, for example. It would be a bad idea to load everything when a lot of the things are currently unnecessary, for example. In scenes, you can design your levels and make them playable.

Now, everything that is present in a scene is called a GameObject (more on these in Chapter 3 of this book). When you make games, you will probably require images, sound, 3D models, etc. All of what you import in your project is an asset, whether you ever use it in a scene.

I'll go through some of the most frequently used windows in Unity. Your empty project should look mostly like this (Figure 2-7):

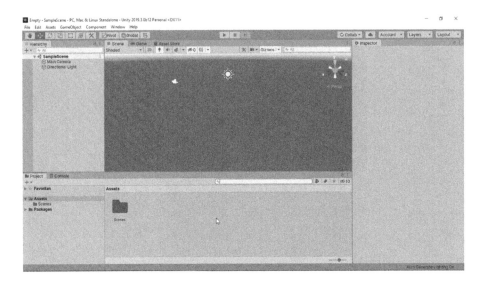

Figure 2-7. *An empty scene*

You can change the layout of these windows by clicking the little layout button found at the top right of the Unity Editor (Figure 2-8). You can also resize them by dragging their edges.

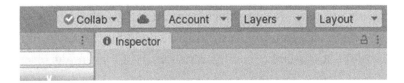

Figure 2-8. *Layouts*

2.3.1 The Project Window

If you're using the default layout, it should normally be found at the bottom of the editor. The Project window (Figure 2-9) is a collection of assets and directories that you have created or imported into a Unity project. You can also search the entire project to find an asset by its name or type, by using the search bar.

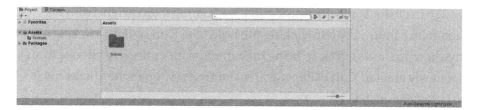

Figure 2-9. *The Project window*

2.3.2 The Hierarchy Window

The Hierarchy window (Figure 2-10) basically contains a list of all the game objects that are present in the scene that is currently opened inside the editor. By default, it contains a camera and a light source, which you'll learn more about in Chapter 3. It is found at the top left of the editor, in the default layout.

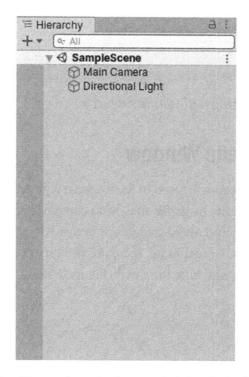

Figure 2-10. *The Hierarchy window, as it is by default*

Try to create some primitive and basic GameObjects right from the Hierarchy window, by left-clicking the little plus icon or right-clicking anywhere in the window, to bring up a menu with options to choose from. The newly created GameObject will instantly show up in the Hierarchy window (Figure 2-11).

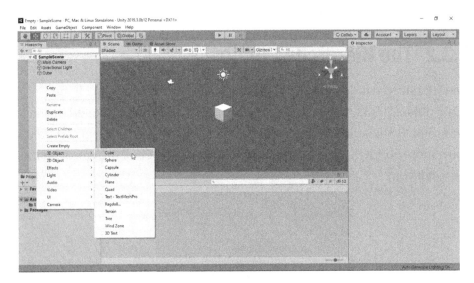

Figure 2-11. *Creating a 3D GameObject*

2.3.3 The Scene Window

The Scene window is mostly used in level design where GameObjects must be placed to create in-game areas. You can navigate around the scene by using your mouse and make changes directly to objects in the scene in the Scene window. Note that the red color designates the x axis, green designates the y axis, and blue the z axis (Figure 2-12).

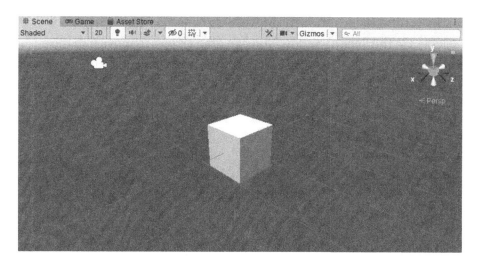

Figure 2-12. *The scene window with a cube*

You can select objects by left-clicking them in the Scene window. Try also right-clicking and dragging to rotate around, or use the scroll wheel to zoom in and out. You can finally click and hold the scroll wheel and move your mouse to pan around. If you left-click and select objects in the Inspector window, they will appear selected in the Scene window also.

There are seven tools (Figure 2-13) to help you perform operations in the Scene view. The first is the Hand tool. When it is selected, no object will be selected when you click them. Instead, the left mouse button will be used to pan around the scene in the same way that holding the scroll wheel does, as previously described.

Figure 2-13. *The seven scene tools*

The second scene tool is the Move tool (Figure 2-14). When an object is selected in the Scene window, you can drag arrows to move it in the direction of a specific axis. The object may also be dragged by the two little squares, to move along two axes simultaneously.

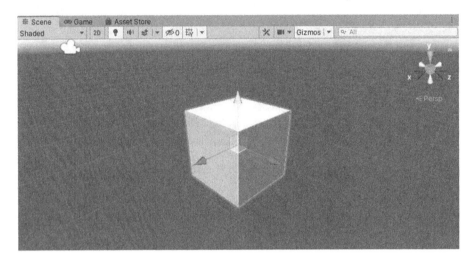

Figure 2-14. *The Move tool*

The third scene tool, the Rotate tool, works in the same way as the Move tool, except that it is used for rotating GameObjects. By dragging along the colored circles, you can rotate a GameObject on one of the three axes, or along the gray circles, to rotate on two axes simultaneously (Figure 2-15).

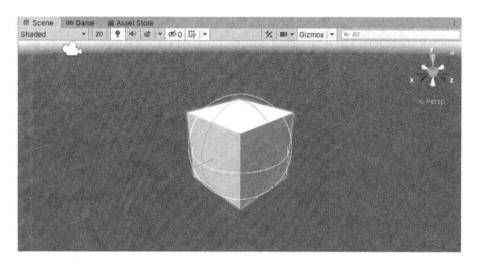

Figure 2-15. *The Rotate tool*

The fourth tool is the Scale tool (Figure 2-16), which allows us to scale selected GameObjects down or up. By dragging along the colored squares, you're scaling GameObjects up or down along the respective axis, and by dragging from the little square at the center of the GameObject, you're scaling GameObjects up or down uniformly along all axes at a time.

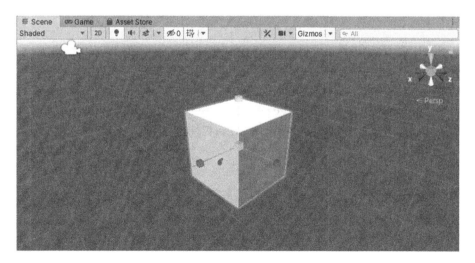

Figure 2-16. *The Scale tool*

The fifth scene tool is the Rect tool, which is useful for moving and scaling 2D objects. We'll be using it afterward, when we'll have to move or scale images, buttons, and 2D UI elements.

The sixth tool combines the features of the Move, Rotate, and Scale tools. We'll skip what it does and use the seventh and final (Multi) tool for now (Figure 2-17).

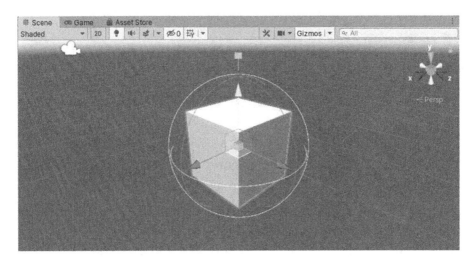

Figure 2-17.   *The Multi tool*

In the Scene view, you can also click the little cones at the top-right corner of the window, to make the view angle perpendicular to an axis. For example, try clicking the red cone, to make the view angle perpendicular to the x axis, and, essentially, the content you see will now appear in two dimensions, bounded by the z and y axes (Figure 2-18).

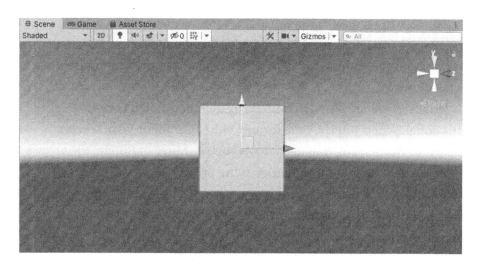

Figure 2-18. *Viewing in the x axis direction*

You can also click the text under the little cones, to switch between a perspective or orthographic view, depending on the type of game you're making.

The first button at the top left of the Scene view allows you to see GameObjects in another form. A good example of moving to wireframe could be to adjust wheels for a car (Figure 2-19).

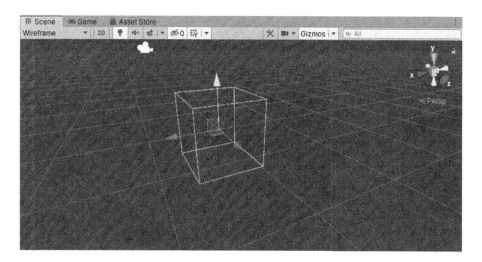

Figure 2-19. *Wireframe shading in the Scene window*

The little 2D button at the top of the window makes everything appear in 2D, which is useful for working with 2D UI elements or on 2D games. The other buttons mainly serve to toggle on or off such things as lighting, audio, or effects.

Finally, there are also two buttons by default, labeled Center and Global. When you click the former, either Center or Pivot will be displayed. When using transform tools such as Move or Rotate, the arrows will be placed either at the center or at the pivot point of the selected GameObject(s). Try this in the Editor now, to get more comfortable with working with these. Try moving, rotating, and scaling 3D objects, and practice everything you've learned until now.

For example, if there are two cubes in the scene and both have been selected, if the first button is set to Center, the current tool will be placed equidistant from the two cubes (Figure 2-20).

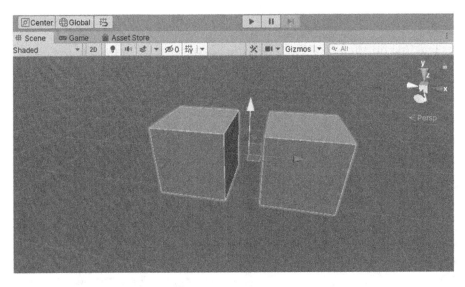

Figure 2-20. *Center point of two GameObjects*

If Pivot is used instead, the tool will be placed at the center of one of the two cubes, therefore known as the pivot point. In this case, the pivot point will be determined by which of the two cubes is selected first. If the left one is selected first, its center will be the pivot point (Figure 2-21).

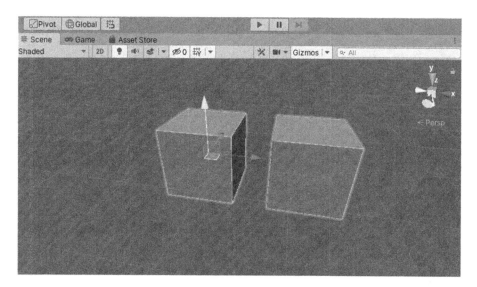

Figure 2-21. *Pivot point of two GameObjects*

Now on to Global and Local modes. Basically, when the mode of the first button is set to Global, all the tools will have the same positioning relative to the world. The red arrow will always point right (x axis); the green arrow will always point up (y axis); and the blue arrow will always point forward (z axis). These won't depend on the position, rotation, or scale of the selected GameObject(s).

However, for the Local mode, the tool will always depend on the position, rotation, or scale of the selected GameObject(s). In a way, it's like saying the blue arrow "is the z axis of the GameObject," which means that the blue arrow will point to the forward movement of the GameObject(s), rather than the norm, which is across the world space that Global defines. In the following example, the cube is slightly rotated, so that its "forward" points a bit upward (Figure 2-22).

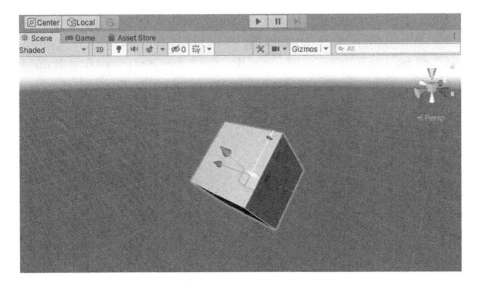

Figure 2-22. *Local mode with a selected GameObject*

There is also a little magnet icon next to the Global/Local button. This can be used to toggle on/off Grid Snapping. This can be used when tool positioning is set to Global. Grid Snapping allows you to move objects by units of 1 across all axes and will thus snap the position of GameObject(s) to the closest whole number position in the scene.

2.3.4 Game View

This can be found just beside the Scene window, if you're using the default layout. It is mostly used for testing game projects before exporting, as it shows a representation of the actual exported game to a third-party user (Figure 2-23).

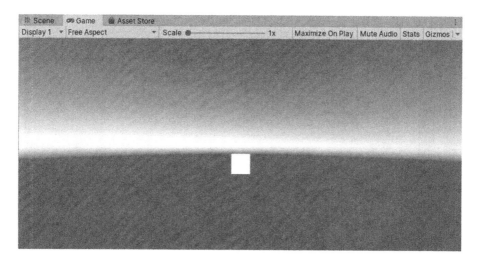

Figure 2-23. *The game view*

Figure 2-23 shows what your empty game would look like if someone tried to play it right now. Display 1 allows you to toggle between different displays, to see how specific places will look.

The Free Aspect tab allows you to set a resolution/ratio, so that it is easier for you to see how the game will be rendered on a display with that particular resolution/ratio. Free Aspect takes the whole size of the game window. You can also create new resolutions or ratios (Figure 2-24).

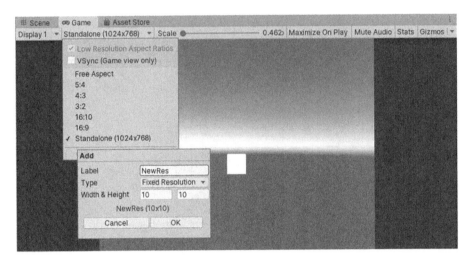

Figure 2-24. *Setting a new resolution/ratio in the Game view*

Using the slider for scale, you can zoom in or out of the Game window, although that is not available in the actual game if you don't implement something similar. Maximize On Play can be set on or off. It will appear whiter if activated, and that allows you to test your game in full screen. Note that at this point, nothing will happen if you toggle it on or off.

Stats allow you to preview some info about the game, such as CPU usage or the number of vertices present (Figure 2-25).

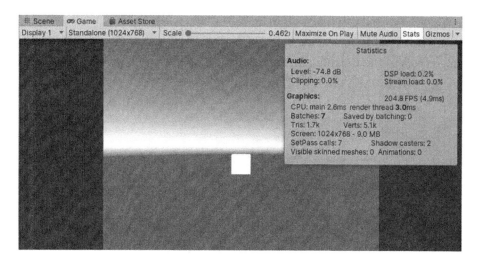

Figure 2-25. *Showing stats in the Game view*

Gizmos allows you to preview more things that are shown to the end user, such as components like colliders, which you'll learn more about in the next chapters. Finally, on to Play mode.

When you want to test your game without exporting a build of it, you can do that within the editor. There are three icons at the top of the Game window. The first (leftmost) one is the Play button. When you click that button, the Editor goes darker, the button turns blue, and you're in what is called Play mode. In Play mode, you're playing the game as a normal user would if they had a build of that game. To exit Play mode, you simply click the Play button again.

When in Play mode (Figure 2-26), you can click the button beside it—the Pause button to temporarily pause the game. Clicking the Pause button again will resume it. The last (rightmost) button is the Step button, and whenever you click it, it will automatically play one frame and pause the game, if it isn't paused already. You can still click the Pause button to resume the game. The Step button is useful if we want to know what's happening with each frame that is leading to a bug.

Please be aware that any changes you make while in Play mode are temporary. That is, if, for example, you move an object in Play mode, when you go back to the normal editing mode, the changes will revert to how they were before you entered Play mode.

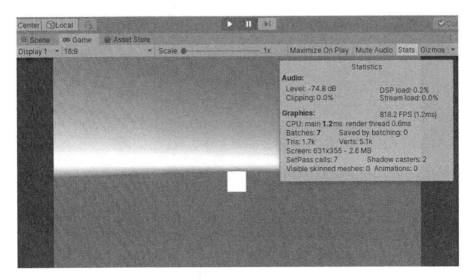

Figure 2-26. *Entering Play mode*

2.3.5 The Inspector Window

If you're using the default layout, the Inspector is the big vertical triangle at the right side of your screen. It contains much information on selected GameObject(s), based on the components that are attached to this (these) GameObject(s). By default, all GameObjects have a transform component (Figures 2-27 and 2-28). Most components have fields or properties with values that can be tweaked from this window.

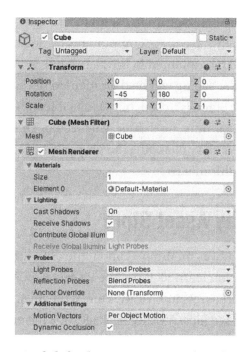

Figure 2-27. *A typical default Inspector window for a cube: part 1*

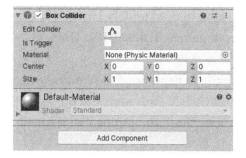

Figure 2-28. *A typical default Inspector window for a cube: part 2*

The cube we've been taking as an example, or a new cube that we create, should normally have these components by default. The purpose of tags and layers will be explained in the last chapters, and the use of the components you're seeing will be documented in Chapter 3. When the check box next to Static is ticked, our GameObject(s) won't move or physically change at runtime, no matter what we do. This has performance gains. You are advised to try changing the properties of some components, to see the difference this makes.

2.3.6 The Unity Asset Store

If you remember what was mentioned about the definition of assets in the section where you learned about the Project window, there are several ways to import assets into Unity. One of the most common is by opening `.unitypackage` files. A Unity package, or a file ending with a `.unitypackage` extension, is a compressed file that includes several assets.

For this section, we'll focus mostly on downloading and importing assets from the Asset Store, rather than from third-party unofficial sources. The Asset Store is kind of marketplace where you can browse and download assets for your games. Think of it as Unity's Google Play for Assets.

To access the Asset Store, you must head to Window and click the Asset Store tab. Or simply hit Ctrl+9. You can resize the Asset Store window or place it somewhere. It should look something like Figure 2-29 in full screen.

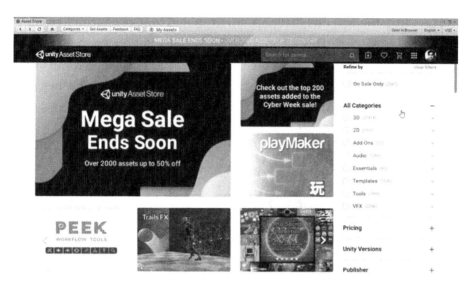

Figure 2-29. *The Asset Store*

You can search for assets using the search bar and use filters for things such as price and category. For the sake of this tutorial, we are going to download and import a package called Simple Input, which happens to be free. Use the pricing filter to target only free assets (Figure 2-30).

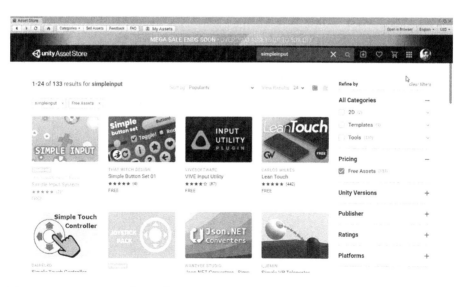

Figure 2-30. *Searching for assets*

Then click the first one that pops up (it should look like the first result in the preceding screenshot). You can read the description, preview what files will be imported, and check out the screenshots or reviews while on the page of an asset. Hit download when you're ready. When it finishes downloading, you should now see on that button that Import appears instead of Download (Figure 2-31). Click it.

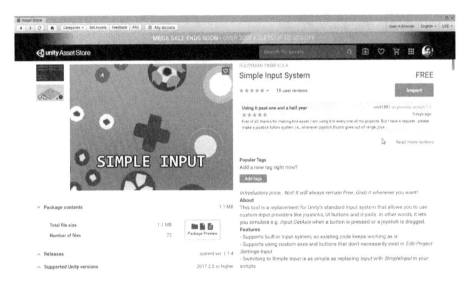

Figure 2-31.   *The Simple Input system asset*

Unity will now decompress the package. Finally, hit Import. The assets will appear in your Project window once everything is imported (Figure 2-32).

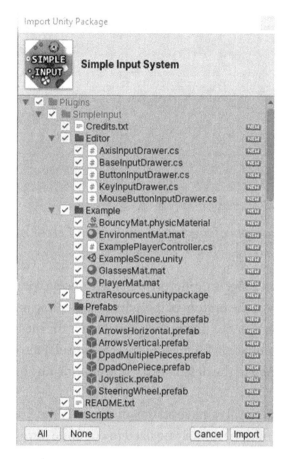

Figure 2-32. *Importing an asset—Simple Input System in our project*

2.3.7 The Console Window

Console is a read-only window that can have logs, warnings, or errors (Figure 2-33). While testing your code for your game projects, you'll often output values to the Console, to make sure everything is working as expected. This is called debugging. Unity may also warn you of things that may not really affect your project right now but can cause problems in the long term. As for errors, you must fix them; otherwise, you will not be able to run or build your game.

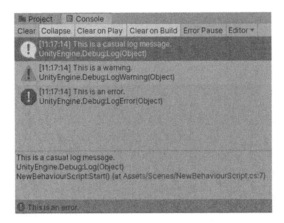

Figure 2-33. *Example of logging, warning, and error messages in the Console*

When you click a log/warning/error in the Console window, more details will appear at the bottom of the screen, indicating mainly the statement and line number that are responsible for the message in question. If you double-click a message in the Console, the responsible script will be opened in the default text/code editor Unity has been assigned to use.

The Clear button will remove all the messages in the Console window, except those that must absolutely be fixed to continue development of your game project (Figure 2-34). The Clear on Play automatically performs the operations of the Clear button every time you enter the Play mode, as long as it is enabled. Similarly, Clear on Build will run each time Unity successfully builds an executable file of your game.

Figure 2-34. *Amount of messages by type and genre in the Console window*

The Collapse tab will compile the same console messages together in a single message. The number of instances will be represented in a small circle at the far right of the Console window. Error Pause will pause the game in Play mode when an error is received, and the last drop-down button Editor allows you to choose where you want to have debug messages from, perhaps from a device connected to your computer, for example.

The Search bar allows you to search for messages in particular, and the last three small colored buttons allow you to choose what kind of debug messages you desire. For example, clicking the yellow button will stop all warning messages from popping in the Console window. However, the number of every type of logging message received since the last time you hit Clear will still continue to be displayed beside their respective buttons.

2.3.8 Build Settings

This can be accessed from File ➤ Build Settings. In the Build Settings window, you can switch to the platform with which you want to export your game and adjust some more options that will be covered more fully in future sections (Figure 2-35). The current platform you're on will be represented by a small Unity logo before its label. For future projects, switch to the Android platform. You'll see how to configure and make builds soon. Drag and drop the scenes you want in the Build Settings window. The first one will be the one the player will see as they open your game. Finally, it's a good practice to save your scene and project. Do so from the File tab.

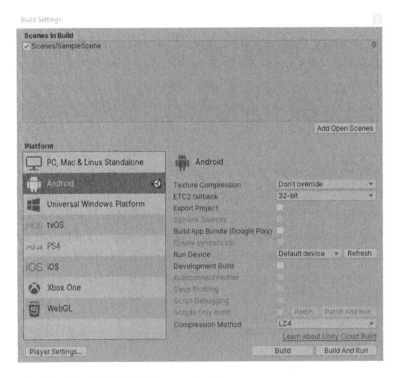

Figure 2-35. *The Build Settings window*

CHAPTER 3

GameObjects, Prefabs, Materials, and Components

As stated in Chapter 2, games built with Unity are usually arranged in scenes. These scenes usually contain many objects to enhance them and make the game interactable and enjoyable. The goal is to have a concrete game with solid mechanics, good gameplay, and good graphics.

3.1 GameObjects and Prefabs

In Unity, objects in scenes are referred to as "GameObjects." When you create a new scene, it contains a Main Camera and a Directional Light. These are GameObjects. Every object you find in the Hierarchy window is a GameObject. If you create a cube, it is also a GameObject.

Now, if you have multiple scenes and are using a common GameObject in all of them, it would be great if you could drag and drop that object in all of them, instead of configuring it from scratch for every scene, right? This is where prefabs come in. You can basically save a version of a GameObject and drag and drop it in other scenes (Figure 3-1). You just have to drag and drop a GameObject in the Project window, and it will turn into a prefab.

© Kishan Takoordyal 2020
K. Takoordyal, *Beginning Unity Android Game Development*,
https://doi.org/10.1007/978-1-4842-6002-9_3

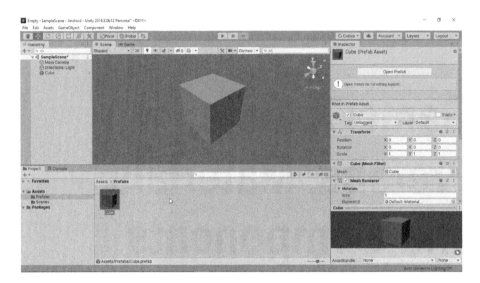

Figure 3-1. *Making prefabs*

The GameObject you just turned into a prefab will now have a bluish tint to it in the Hierarchy tab. As for your prefab, you can just load another scene and drag it into the Hierarchy or Scene tab of that newly opened scene.

You can also make changes directly to a prefab. You just have to double-click it in the Project window. The Scene window will now have a bluish background, and you will now be able to see the children of that prefab (if it had any) and make changes to its properties, as well as to those of its children.

After making the desired changes, you can save them by clicking the little arrow beside the prefab name at the top-left corner of the Hierarchy window, or by using a shortcut such using Ctrl;+S. The former action will automatically save changes made to the prefab and return you to the scene that was previously open. All instances of that prefab will then be updated with these changes in all the scenes in which they are found (Figure 3-2).

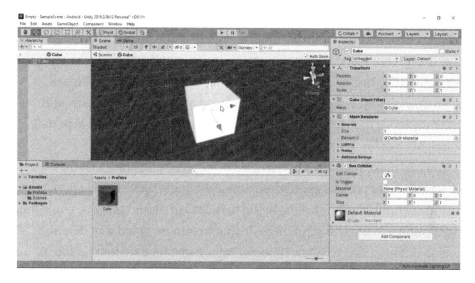

Figure 3-2. *Opening prefabs*

If you make changes to the GameObject that you turned into a prefab in the scene, there is an Overrides button in the Inspector window that you can click to cause the changes you made to be applied to the prefab and thus to every instance of that prefab in other scenes (Figure 3-3). You can also revert properties to those of the prefab version. This is not a necessary step, and you can as well have a GameObject in a scene that comes from a prefab but does not have the exact same properties.

Figure 3-3. *Overriding prefab properties*

If you made a prefab, placed it in a scene, and don't want it to be updated or overridden by future changes made to the prefab, you can always make that prefab instance become an independent GameObject, by right-clicking it in the Inspector and either clicking Unpack Prefab or Unpack Prefab Completely. For example, if you placed a prefab in one scene, and it has properties that completely differ from the ones in the original prefab, you might wish for that version to be completely independent.

You can make prefabs of prefabs, for example, by creating a GameObject that has multiple prefabs as children and itself being turned into a prefab. The former option will just remove the first level of nested prefabs, while the latter option will remove all of them. It should also be noted that deleting a prefab does not delete GameObjects that are instances of that prefab in scenes. These prefab instances will just become independent GameObjects and will have a reddish tint along their names in the Hierarchy (Figure 3-4). Nesting prefabs can be useful in a game in which all enemies behave in a similar way and share the same base features.

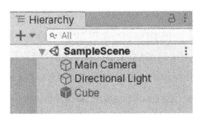

Figure 3-4. *Deleting prefabs*

3.2 Components

Every GameObject has components. A component is basically a module that can be attached to a GameObject. A component provides several new properties and features in addition to those an empty GameObject already provides. Some components require other components to be present on a GameObject to work properly, while some are compulsory, even when you wish to create an empty 3D object. When you select GameObjects, you will see all the common components that are attached to them in the Inspector window that can also be shrunk or expanded by clicking their names (Figure 3-5).

Figure 3-5. *Multiple components*

In the Inspector window, you can change the values of components. You can also click the three dots at the top-right corner of components, in order to bring up more options, such as Reset, which will assign default values to the component, as if you just added it.

You can also copy and paste component values to two components at the same time, by clicking Copy Component. After selecting the GameObject having the component you wish to override the values of, click Paste Component Values. You can also copy components and directly paste them on another GameObject.

It should also be noted that a GameObject can have more than one instance of a particular component, although there are some exceptions to this. You can also reorder components on a GameObject, by dragging them up or down, or by using the three dots and clicking Move Up or Move Down.

Beside the three dots icon, there's another button. Clicking it allows you to use a preset for the respective component.

To get the manual or documentation for a component, you can simply click the question mark icon beside the preset button on the left. A browser tab will open with suitable and relevant information (Figure 3-6).

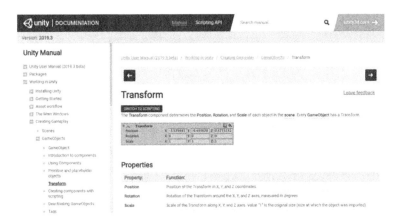

Figure 3-6. *Viewing the documentation*

Finally, you can add new components to a GameObject by clicking the Add Component button and browsing or searching for the component you wish to add, or by using the Editor menu (Figure 3-7).

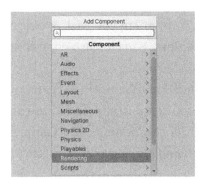

Figure 3-7. *Adding components*

3.2.1 Transform

If you followed along in Chapter 2, you have already interacted with the Transform component from the Scene window and might have a solid idea of what it is about. The Transform component is required by every GameObject. Unlike integer or float data types, the Transform component is made up of three sets of Vector3 values. You can think of a Vector3 as being a float array made up of three values. From the first index, or from the left, these three values are respectively denoted by the "x," "y," and "z" characters. The three sets of Vector3 values of the Transform component are the position, rotation, and scale of the selected GameObject(s) (Figure 3-8).

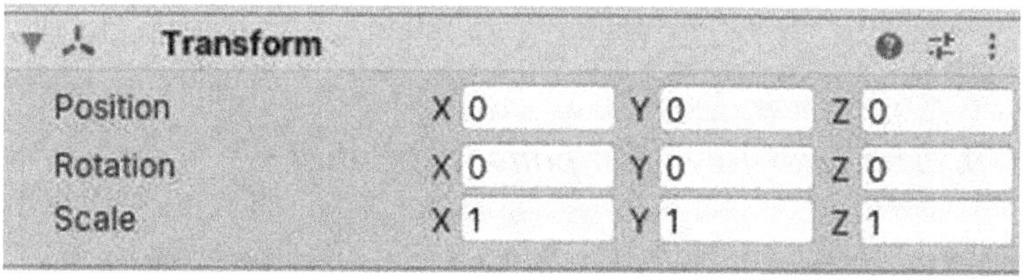

▼ 人 **Transform**						❷ ⇌ ⋮
Position	X	0	Y	0	Z	0
Rotation	X	0	Y	0	Z	0
Scale	X	1	Y	1	Z	1

Figure 3-8. *The Transform component*

The x axis is denoted by the red color and goes from left (-) to right (+) horizontally. The y axis is denoted by the green color and goes from bottom (-) to top (+) vertically, and the z axis is denoted by the blue color and goes from backward (-) to forward (+). All the axes are perpendicular to one another.

The Position Vector3 represents the position of the GameObject in the world in X, Y, and Z values. You can change these values by directly entering them into the text boxes beside the specific axis name, or by dragging your cursor from the axis name to the right (+) or left (-), in the Inspector tab itself.

The Rotation Vector3 represents the rotation of the GameObject in the world in x, y, and z values, and the Scale Vector3 represents the position of the GameObject in the world in x, y, and z values.

However, if the selected GameObject is the child of another GameObject, its position, rotation, and scale is relative to its parent. For example, following are the Transform component of two different cubes (Figures 3-9 and 3-10):

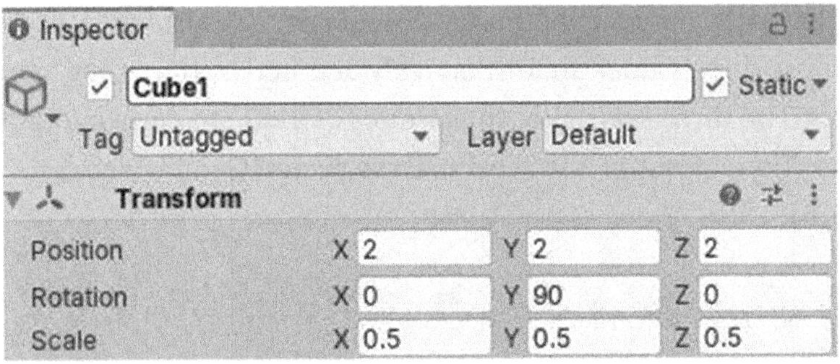

Figure 3-9. *The Transform component of Cube1*

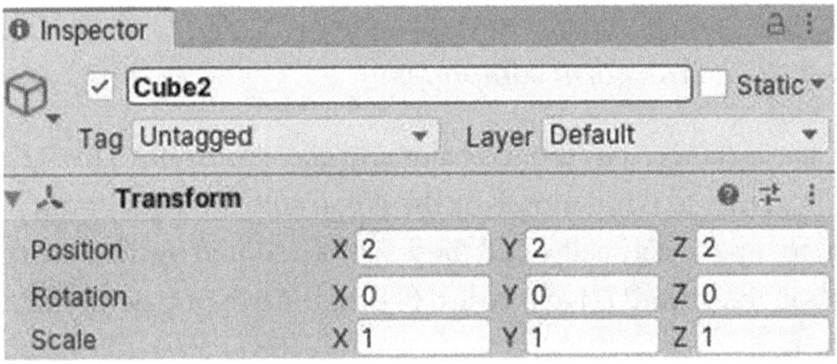

Figure 3-10. *The Transform component of Cube2*

Now, if we had to make Cube2 a child of Cube1, by dragging its GameObject on that of the latter in the Hierarchy window, here is what its transform would look like (Figure 3-11):

● Inspector			a :
✓ **Cube2**			☐ Static ▾
Tag Untagged	▾	Layer Default	▾
▾ ⅄ **Transform**			❷ ⇌ :
Position	X 0	Y 0	Z 0
Rotation	X 0	Y -90	Z 0
Scale	X 2	Y 2	Z 2

Figure 3-11. *The Transform component of Cube2 if it is a child of Cube1*

Because it is at the same position as Cube1, relative to its parent, the Vector3 position of Cube2 will be 0 on all axes. As its rotation is 0 everywhere, for it to maintain that, Cube2 must subtract 90 degrees on its relative y axis, to maintain that value of 0, because Cube1 is rotated by 90 degrees on its own y axis. As for the scale, it's pretty self-explanatory: Cube2 is bigger than Cube1 by two times along all the axes.

3.2.2 Camera

A camera is the equivalent of our eyes in a video game. Everything you perceive in a game is being "seen" by a component known as Camera. Typically, at one particular time, you'd have only one main camera enabled in a single-player game, to show the player what they can see. If you're playing a third-person game, the camera will be behind the main character you're controlling and, thus, create the impression that the latter is being watched and followed by another entity. In a first-person game, the camera acts as the eyes of the character you're controlling.

There should normally be a Camera component already attached to a GameObject (Main Camera) in an empty scene, if you haven't made any modifications to it (Figure 3-12).

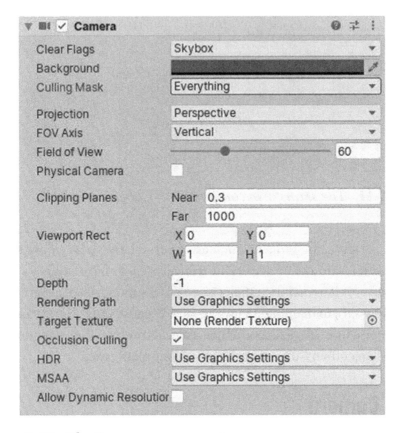

Figure 3-12.   *The Camera component*

The Clear Flags option allows you to choose from a predefined list what should be displayed in empty areas of the camera.

- By default, it is set to Skybox, which, as you will learn later, is made up of a total of six images that usually complement one another to form a sort of cube that surrounds the scene.

- Additionally, you can choose the Solid Color option and pick a color in the Background property just below.

- If you choose Depth Only, nothing will be displayed in empty areas, and Don't Clear will persistently display whatever was present in the last frame, if not overridden by anything.

Culling masks is a mechanism to control what gets rendered to this camera, based on the graphical elements that have been assigned to groups, called Layers.

Next, you can choose whether to make the camera use a perspective or orthographic view. If you choose orthographic (by default, it's perspective), everything the camera sees will be in a somewhat 2D view.

- With an orthographic camera, you have the ability to adjust the size of the camera, i.e., the area that it can "see" at one particular moment or frame.

- With a perspective camera, you have the ability to choose its field of view, which is literally the process of adjusting the "angle" it can "see" from its center.

You can also adjust whether the field of view is along the Horizontal (x) axis, which goes from top to bottom, or along the Vertical (y) axis, which goes from left to right.

Still, for a perspective view, you can choose to make the camera more configurable, by ticking Physical Camera (Figure 3-13). This will allow you to adjust more settings, such as the focal length and the sensor size of the camera. By the way, to change the position and rotation/orientation of the camera, you have to modify the respective values in the Transform component of the GameObject that has that Camera component attached.

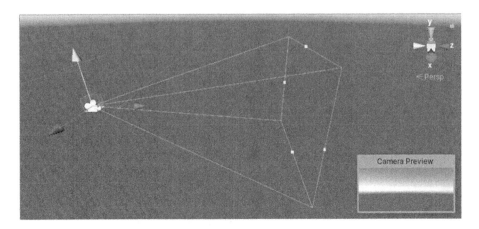

Figure 3-13. *A perspective camera*

Now come the Clipping Planes. Unity's equivalent of 1 unit translates to 1 meter in the real world. For a camera, the Clipping Planes setting has a Near and a Far value. These two values represent the minimum and the maximum distance of a GameObject to a camera for the latter to render it. If the camera is closer than the Near distance to a GameObject, say, the camera is at the very center of the GameObject in question and the Near value is something like 0.5, it won't get rendered. If now another GameObject is way far from the camera at a distance greater than the Far value, it won't get rendered either.

As for the Viewport Rect setting, it is made up of two sets of Vector2 values. As everything displayed on a screen is in 2D form, there isn't a third value for these sets of data to represent the z axis.

- The X and Y values allow you to adjust horizontally and vertically, respectively, where the render of the camera should be positioned.

- The W and H values represent the portion of the screen that will be used for the render of the camera horizontally and vertically, respectively. A value of 1 represents using the full width or height of the screen, and a 0 represents none.

For example, if you were making a console racing game with a split screen feature for two players, you could have two cameras, each taking half of the screen, following one of the two players. Both cameras would have a W value of 0.5, an H value of 0, and a Y value of 0, but a different value of X to match the position of the left and right halves of the screen.

If you are using multiple cameras in a scene, you can set a different depth value for them. For example, if you're making a game in which you can switch between a third-person and first-person view, you can make use of two cameras for either views, but as they both take up 100% of the screen real estate, the depth value determines what camera will be rendered to the player. In that example, the player will see what the camera having the highest depth value is "seeing."

The rest of the settings will have a very brief description, and for simple or small projects, you probably won't have to mess with those, and if you do, it's better edit that of the project itself, rather than individual settings of cameras. The Rendering Path setting allows you to choose how GameObjects are rendered by a camera with respect to lighting.

The Target Texture allows you to assign a 2D render texture to a Camera component. That texture will then be updated with whatever the camera sees in the scene. This is useful for when you want to create a minimap in the form of a bird's-eye view, for example. A camera can be set up to follow the player from above and look down (90, 0, 0). It could then output to a 2D texture that can then be assigned to a "rectangle" that will always be shown in the top-right corner of the screen.

Occlusion Culling is a popular technology that can drastically improve performance in some types of games. If you are making use of that technology and in particular want a camera to benefit from it, tick the respective check box. For Occlusion Culling to work properly, your scene has to be "baked" for this specific feature; otherwise, ticking the check box won't result in any changes.

As for high dynamic range (HDR) and multisampling anti-aliasing (MSAA) rendering, they can make your game look better, but using MSAA, especially, has important performance costs.

Finally, ticking Allow Dynamic Resolution will allow the camera to scale render textures, if the platform you're building your game for supports it.

3.2.3 Lighting

Lighting is very important in a video game. The position and rotation of a main light determines the portion of GameObjects that are visible, relative to their angle to the direction rays are cast from the light source and, thus, the direction that shadows are cast, as well as the size of these.

An empty scene in Unity will by default have a GameObject known as a Directional Light, with a Light component (Figure 3-14) that provides uniform light in a single direction, simulating something similar to a sun. If there were no light sources in a scene, the world would be completely dark.

In the Hierarchy window, you can create from four default types of light sources, namely, Directional, Point, Spot, and Area. A Directional light can be used to light a scene entirely and basically act as the sun. Point lights are used for more niche scenarios, such as, for example, torches in a medieval village. Spot lights can be used, for example, to simulate flashlights in a dark house for a horror game, and Area lights can be used to uniformly light up a defined area.

To keep this part simple, I will be basing explanations on Directional light sources only. The additional settings that are obtained with the other types of light sources are fairly self-explanatory.

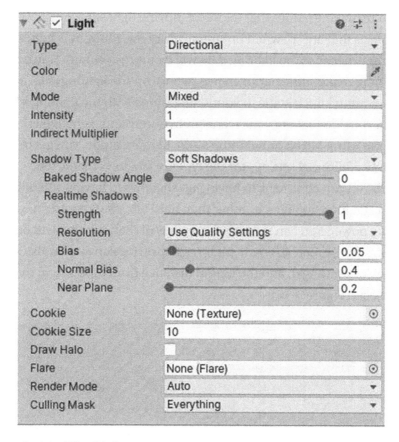

Figure 3-14. *The Light component*

First, you can set the color of the light to be emitted by the light source. You can then set the light mode to Realtime, Mixed, or Baked.

- If you're using the Realtime light mode, GameObjects will be shaded as you play the game.

- With Baked, you can "bake" your scene to make a type of lighting data asset that will be assigned to that light source automatically.

- If you're using Mixed, you will have a combination of Baked and Realtime lighting.

If you're making games that require a moving light source or have GameObjects that are spawned progressively or randomly, it is better to use Realtime, because the lighting data will be more accurate. However, if you want to make some performance savings on the lighting side, and if objects are pretty much static in your scene, along with the lighting source, you might consider baking your scene prematurely and using Baked.

If you're using Mixed or Realtime as the lighting mode, you get to tweak some additional settings for the types of shadows that will be produced. You can choose from having no shadows to having soft or hard ones. Soft shadows appear smoother than hard ones but require more processing power. You can then modify values of shadows that will be produced, such as their strength, their resolution (which can be also set in the project's settings), and the bias in distance from their respective GameObjects (Figure 3-15).

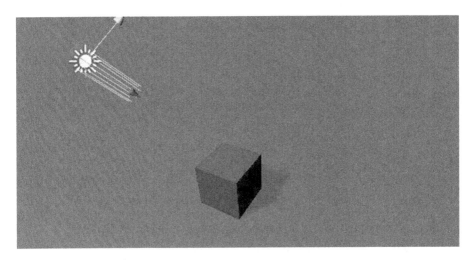

Figure 3-15. *Quite normal intensity light on a cube*

You can also increase or decrease the intensity and indirect multiplier of a light source. Indirect light is light that gets reflected by one GameObject on another GameObject. Increasing either of these two values makes the scene appear brighter. Here's what the scene in the preceding figure would look like if the intensity of the light source were bumped to twice its original value (Figure 3-16):

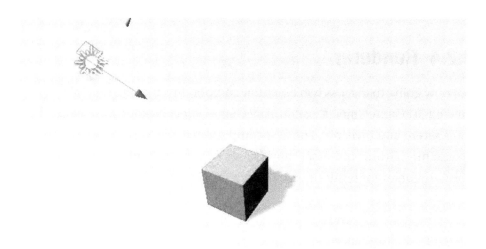

Figure 3-16. *High-intensity light on a cube*

The cookie property allows you to assign a 2D texture to the light source. The texture will be used as a mask. You can think of it as being a thick cardboard shape (in the form of a dinosaur, maybe) that's brought in front of a light source (a bulb). This will define the shadows, silhouettes, or patterns that will be obtained when light from the source is cast. You can also edit the size of that cookie mask in the option just below it.

Ticking Draw Halo will create a blurry sphere around the light source, with a radius equal to its range (a property available if you're using point or spot light sources) and of the same color as the light cast by the source.

Flare can be used to allow flares to be rendered by the light source in the scene, which might be useful if you're making cinematics. The Render Mode can be changed to reflect the importance of lights in a scene, if you're using some form of Forward Rendering. Finally, in a manner similar to that for cameras, you can select layers of GameObjects that will be affected by the light source in its Culling Mask property. GameObjects of Layers not selected won't be affected in any way by that light source. In Unity's documentation, you can find additional details on different light samples.

3.2.4 Renderer

I'm now going to discuss two essential components that are crucial to making 3D GameObjects visible. Any GameObject lacking these would be transparent and invisible. The first component is the Mesh Filter, which takes a mesh from your assets and passes it to the second component, the Mesh Renderer for rendering on the screen (Figure 3-17).

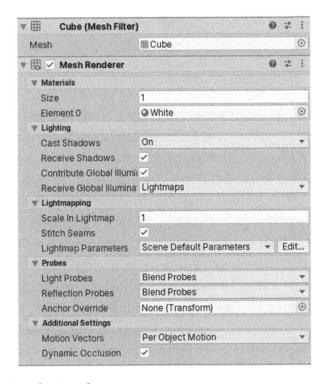

Figure 3-17. *The Renderer component*

In further topics, you'll be learning what exactly materials are, but for now, just assume they're colors.

A Renderer can make use of multiple materials, depending on how the mesh from the Mesh Filter component is set up. The lighting properties can be tweaked, if you want to customize how a GameObject receives or casts shadows.

You probably won't need to mess with the other properties of Renderers when making games, but you can always access Unity's documentation or manual to learn more.

3.2.5 Collider

Physics in a game depends on Rigidbodies and colliders. Colliders are the group of components that allow collision to occur. It is also common to see colliders being used as triggers. For example, getting sufficiently close to a nonplayer character (NPC) in a game may trigger a dialogue between the NPC and your character.

In Unity, there are six types of colliders natively, mainly

- Box (Figure 3-18)

- Sphere

- Capsule

- Mesh

- Wheel

- Terrain

In this book, I will cover the first four colliders. Wheel colliders are used to make the wheels of land vehicles, among other similar objects, and Terrain colliders are used with terrains, which are another form of native 3D object, but with more configurable options. Terrains won't be covered in this book.

▼ 📦 ☑ **Box Collider**			❓ ⇄ ⋮
Edit Collider	🗗		
Is Trigger	☐		
Material	None (Physic Material)		⊙
Center	X 0	Y 0	Z 0
Size	X 1	Y 1	Z 1

Figure 3-18. *The Box Collider component*

Cubes that are created in the Editor come with a Box Collider by default (Figure 3-19). If you click the Edit Collider button, you will have the ability to scale the collider in your scene view. You only have to drag in the direction you wish to scale the collider the little squares that appear.

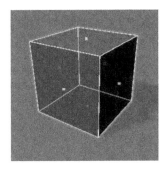

Figure 3-19. *Modifying the bounds of a Box Collider in the scene*

In the Inspector window, changing the x, y, or z value of Vector3, known as "Center" is going to move the collider in the respective direction. Changing values of Size will make the collider bigger or smaller, respective of the axis on which you're modifying its value. It should be noted that increasing or decreasing the scale transform for a GameObject will make its collider's size decrease by a similar ratio. For example, if you create a cube and make all of its scale Vector3 values equal to 2, even if the size of its collider will be 1 on all axes, assuming you didn't manually modify anything, the collider will still wrap around the full volume or size of the cube.

The Physics Material tab just above can be used to make the collider simulate a particular real material. For example, some physics materials can make a collider feel more slippery when you walk on it, such as ice, while others can make it feel like something that appears to have more friction, such asphalt, for example.

If we want an event to fire when two physics objects collide but not have them bounce off each other, trigger colliders are used. So, if you want a light to turn on as you move over a part of the floor, these will help. If you tick IsTrigger on a Collider component, the GameObject associated with it will appear to lack the ability to participate in collisions. In other words, you will be able to walk through the GameObject, even if it has a Collider component when its IsTrigger box is ticked. This is useful when you want to make trigger zones, for example, in a game where walking in an area triggers something to occur, such as playing a cutscene.

The properties of Sphere Colliders (Figure 3-20) are very similar to those of Box Colliders. The only difference is that they have a Radius property instead of a Vector3-size one. You can modify the collider in the Scene window with the first button of that property, but dragging a point will increase the radius uniformly along all axes.

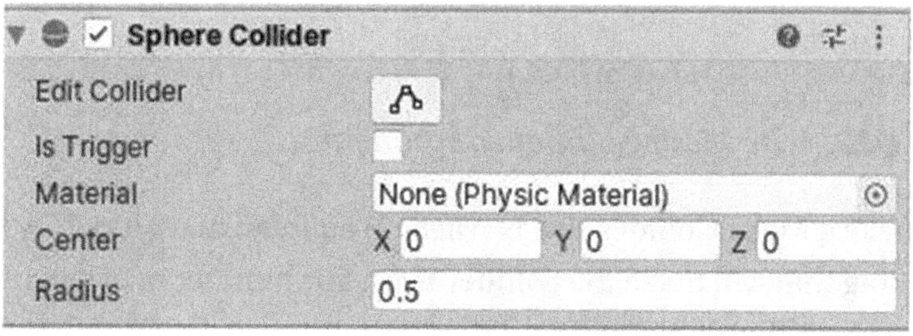

Figure 3-20. *The Sphere Collider component*

Capsules are made up of two semi-spheres (two halves of a sphere), with one found at the top and one at the bottom of the capsule. There is a distance between those two semi-spheres, known as the height. Capsule Colliders similarly have properties for these (Figure 3-21).

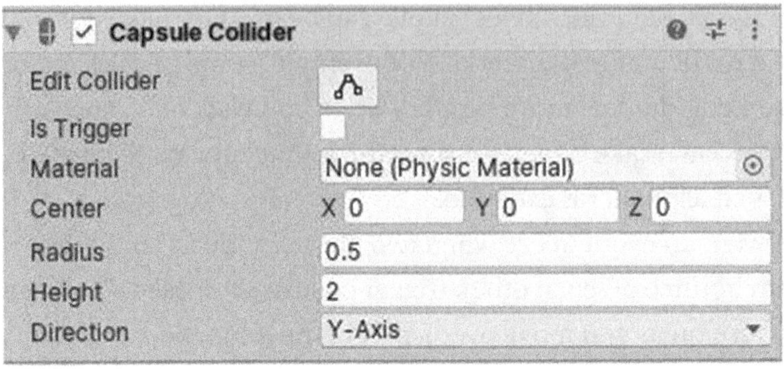

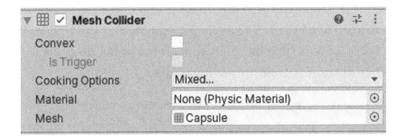

Figure 3-21. The Capsule Collider component

Finally, let's talk about Mesh Colliders (Figure 3-22). If, for example, you have a GameObject that is irregularly shaped, you can add a Mesh Collider component to it. The Mesh Collider will by default add collision to the entire surface of the GameObject.

Figure 3-22. The Mesh Collider component

To make a Mesh Collider, use IsTrigger. You must mark it as "Convex" first. Ticking that will make the collider use a fair number of 3D regular shapes to cover the whole surface area and volume of the GameObject. Using Convex also allows collision between other GameObjects using a Mesh Collider. As far as possible, however, it is recommended that you use the other colliders discussed previously, rather than these, because they offer a performance boost, even if the Mesh Collider is marked as Convex.

3.2.6 Rigidbody

The Rigidbody component (Figure 3-23), which is usually used with a Collider component, is that one magical component that can turn a GameObject into an object that reflects the properties of objects in the real world. It can enable the Physics engine to allow objects to bounce off other objects and simulate such things as gravity. If you're making a game that has to do with physics, you'll very likely have to make use of Rigidbody.

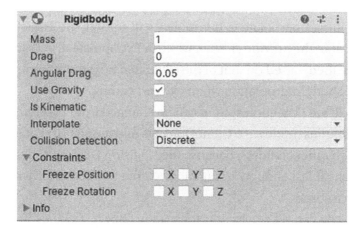

Figure 3-23. *The Rigidbody component*

The Mass property allows you to set the mass of an object. One unit is equivalent to 1 kilogram. Bigger values will make a GameObject feel heavier. Increasing mass will additionally make GameObjects less reactive to external forces (for example, explosions) and fall faster, if using Gravity.

Drag is the equivalent of air resistance, and the difference in this value is seen when making the GameObject fall from a height. Angular Drag is nearly the same, but it can be defined by how much air resistance will affect the GameObject's rotation from torque. A value of 0 for either of these values can be translated as "this GameObject is not affected by air resistance."

Not ticking Use Gravity will prevent the GameObject from falling down automatically, if left at a height above the ground with nothing below supporting it.

If Is Kinematic is ticked, the GameObject will not be affected by normal physics. In order to make the GameObject move or affect its position or rotation, you must manipulate its respective Transform values. This is useful for making moving platforms.

Interpolation can be used to make the GameObject feel smoother, if there's jerkiness in the movement of the player character of a game, for example. Setting Interpolate to Interpolate will smooth the Transform, based on that of the previous frame, while in Extrapolate, the Transform will be smoothed, based on that of the estimated next movement. You'll learn more about Interpolation when we start coding.

The Collision Detection system can be changed from Discrete to one of the Continuous modes, if a GameObject is moving so fast that it's able to go through other colliders, because the Collision Detection system isn't detecting it fast enough. Using modes other than Discrete will have performance costs.

Finally, you can set constraints for a GameObject. Ticking either check box will not allow the GameObject to move or rotate on the respective axis/axes. This doesn't mean that it won't via code or script. It just means that normal physics applied to the Rigidbody (e.g., a collision) won't have any effects to it.

3.2.7 Audio Source and Listener

An Audio Listener component is usually found on the main Camera GameObject. It implements a microphone-like device. It records the sounds around it and plays them through the player's speakers. You can only have one listener in a scene. For example, if at one point in your scene you had a car motor running and producing sound, the sound would play at a higher volume when the camera got closer to it.

In contrast, an Audio Source component is what defines what sound(s) to play and how to play it (them). The position of where the sound is coming from will be determined by the position of the GameObject to which the Audio Source component is attached (Figure 3-24).

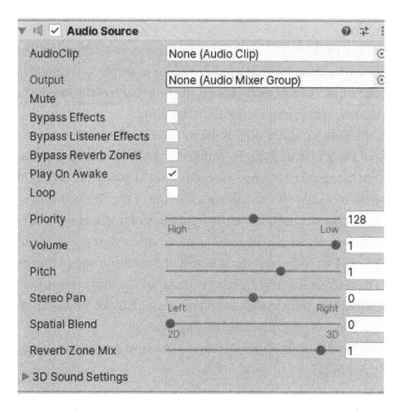

Figure 3-24. *The Audio Source component*

The first property of an Audio Source component is the AudioClip. This is usually an audio file that in Unity you import as an asset. The Audio Mixer Group is another component or asset you can use to further personalize the quality of sound that will be produced.

Ticking Mute disables Audio Listeners from picking up the audio produced by its Audio Source. Later, you can tick bypasses, to prevent the sound produced by the Audio Source from being affected by other effects,

83

either Listener ones or those resulting from another type of component, with Reverb Zones applied to it accordingly.

Play On Awake will make the Audio Source play the assigned Audio Clip as soon as the scene loads, and Loop will make the Audio Source replay the Audio Clip from scratch, each time it has completed playing automatically.

If you have multiple Audio Sources in a scene, you can set a different priority for each, using its Priority slider. If, for example, an Audio Listener is equidistant from two Audio Sources, the one that has the lowest Priority slider of the two will sound louder than the other.

What the Volume slider does is pretty obvious. An Audio Source with a volume of 1 will play its assigned Audio Clip as loud as the maximum volume that the speaker has been set to output at. Note that the sound produced by an Audio Source having a volume of 0 won't be heard.

The Pitch slider is used to set the frequency of the sound produced by an Audio Source. It can also be used to speed up or slow down the sound.

The Stereo Pan slider sets the amount of the output signal that gets routed to Reverb Zones. The amount is linear in the (0–1) range, but allows for a 10 dB amplification in the (1–1.1) range, which can be useful to achieve the effect of near-field and distant sounds.

Spatial Blend, Reverb Zone Mix, and 3D sound settings are beyond the scope of this book.

3.2.8 Particle System

A Particle System is a component that appears to emit some kind of particle or shape at a particular position and rotation (Figure 3-25). For example, using a Particle System may help you to emulate fire, snow, or simply smoke coming from a car's exhaust.

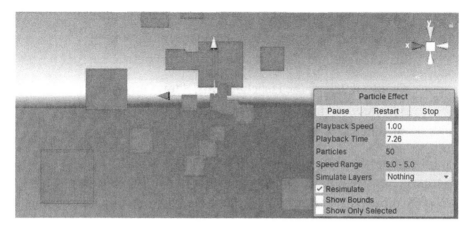

Figure 3-25. *Particle System in a scene*

In your Scene window, a Particle System by default will look something like the preceding screenshot. The three buttons will, respectively, from the left, pause, restart, or stop the Particle System. The difference between Stop and Pause is that Stop will restart the system but pause it immediately.

- Playback Speed can be changed to view the Particle System running at a speed other than that specified.

- Playback Time contains a value that represents the number of seconds that have passed since the Particle System has started running.

- Particles is the number of generated particles that is currently active for that Particle System, and Speed Range is the min-max value for the speed of these particles.

- Simulate Layers allows you to simulate the Particle System on layers other than those of the GameObject that holds it.

- Ticking Resimulate will make changes applied to the Particle System show immediately.

- Show Bounds will make a 3D volume appear in the Scene window, which will indicate the maximum distance that particles can travel in that system.

- Finally, if ticked, the last check box, Show Only Selected, will hide all unselected Particle Systems in the current effect.

Duration (see Figure 3-26) defines the amount of time a Particle System will be emitting. This means that after that number of seconds has passed, no more particles or shapes will be created. Of course, if Looping is ticked, that value doesn't hold any importance, because, then, the system will always keep on emitting.

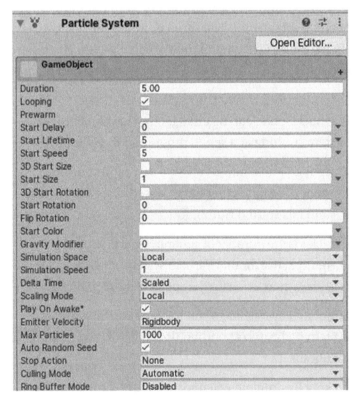

Figure 3-26. *The first settings in a Particle System component*

Start Delay is the amount of time the system will wait before it starts emitting. Start Lifetime defines after how many seconds a particle will be automatically destroyed after it is emitted. Start Speed is the speed at which a particle will travel initially when it is emitted.

Start Size or 3D Start Size can be used to define the size of a particle. Start Rotation or 3D Start Rotation defines its rotation. Flip Rotation can be used to flip the rotation of particles. Start Color changes the color of the particle when it is created.

Gravity Modifier can create particles affected by gravity. A value higher than 0 will make the particles fall down quicker. A value lower than 0 will act according to the previous statement, but the particles will go up instead of down, and 0 will render the particles entirely unaffected by gravity.

Simulation Space can be set to Local, World, or Custom.

- If set to Local, particles will move relative to the Transform of the GameObject their Particle System is attached to.

- In World, they move relative to the world or scene.

- In Custom, you can specify another Transform to make the system relative to.

Simulation Speed is the multiplier at which the Particle System will play back. Changing the Delta Time mode is useful for playing effects while Paused, if using the Unscaled option.

Scaling Mode serves to resize particles relative to the entire hierarchy, local particle node, or only apply scale to the shape.

Ticking Play On Awake will make the particle system start running automatically.

Emitter Velocity allows you to change the mode either to Transform or Rigidbody, depending on how to calculate velocity if the system is moving.

Max Particles defines the maximum number of particles in the system at one particular moment. If this number is reached, no more particles will be emitted until there are fewer particles than the number defined.

Ticking Auto Random Seed will make the simulation different each time the effect is played.

In Stop Action, you can define what to do if the Particle System is stopped and all particles have been destroyed. You can, for example, choose to disable the Particle System component or destroy the GameObject that has the latter as component.

Culling Mode defines what happens when the system is offscreen, i.e., when the particles are not visible onscreen.

- The Catch-up mode pauses offscreen simulations but performs a large simulation step when they become visible, giving the appearance that they were never paused.

- Automatic uses Pause mode for looping systems and AlwaysSimulate if not.

- AlwaysSimulate will never Pause the simulations, even if offscreen.

When Ring Buffer Mode is set to Enabled, particles remain alive until the Max Particles buffer is full, at which point new particles will replace the oldest, instead of dying when their lifetime has elapsed.

I will be discussing Emission (Figure 3-27) and Shape in detail, but for most of the other properties that remain, I will state only what they are used for. A Particle System does not have to make use of all the properties that are available in the Inspector.

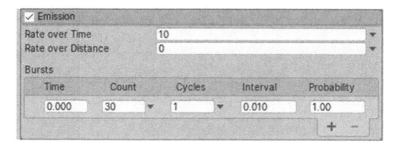

Figure 3-27. *Emission property of the Particle System component*

The value in the Rate over Time property represents the amount of particles that will be emitted per second. That in Rate over Distance is the same as Rate over Time but acts per unit second instead.

The Bursts array allows you to emit particles at specific time frames. Its Time property lets you choose when to emit bursts of particles, and Count designates the number of these particles to emit. Additionally, you can set a curve or create a range for the number of particles to emit, by choosing another setting in the drop-down other than the value.

The value in Cycles allows specifying how many times to repeat the burst. You can set it to infinity by choosing that property when accessing its drop-down menu.

Interval lets you repeat that burst every x seconds, and Probability is a value from 0 to 1. If Probability is set to 0, the burst will never occur, and if set to 1, it will always occur. A value of 0.5 will have the burst occur 50% of the time or not occur 50% of the time.

You can add more sets of values by clicking the plus icon below or remove sets by clicking the minus icon.

Shape represents the 3D volume of the emitter (Figure 3-28). A Spherical shape, for example, will cause particles to be emitted in all directions. We will be looking at the Cone shape for this part. The different options the other shapes provide are quite easy to understand too.

Shape						
Shape	Cone					▾
Angle	25					
Radius	1					
Radius Thickness	1					
Arc	360					
Mode	Random					▾
Spread	0					
Length	5					
Emit from:	Base					▾
Texture	None (Texture 2D)					⊙
Position	X	0	Y	0	Z	0
Rotation	X	0	Y	0	Z	0
Scale	X	1	Y	1	Z	1
Align To Direction	☐					
Randomize Direction	0					
Spherize Direction	0					
Randomize Position	0					

Figure 3-28.   Shape property of the Particle System component

A higher value of Angle will make emitted particles go in more directions, and increasing the Radius will increase the volume that particles can cover. Radius Thickness can have a value from 0 to 1. A value of 0 will make emitted particles seemingly have a denser value.

The value in Arc represents the maximum angle from the center of the emitter from which particles can be spawned. A value of 0 will make particles emit from the center of the emitter only, while a value of 360 allows particles to be emitted at any point along the area of the base of the emitter. For example, as we are using a cone, a value of 360 makes particles spawn at any point found on the small circle that forms the base of the emitter.

Mode allows you to choose how particles are spawned around the Arc. A mode of Random makes them spawn at any position with respect to the original Arc value, and Spread lets you choose to spawn particles at specific angles. A value of 0 disables this behavior.

The value that Emit from uses can be changed to specify from where you want particles to be emitted, either from the Base or the Volume itself. Using a Texture 2D asset, you can modify from where particles will sample their color.

The Vector3 Position allows you to move the emitter volume from the position of the Transform of its GameObject. Rotation and Scale play a similar role.

Ticking Align To Direction will automatically aligns particles, based on their initial direction of travel.

Randomize Direction takes a value of 0 to 1. A value of 1 will override the initial direction of travel of particles with a random direction.

Similarly, Spherize Direction overrides that initial direction of travel with a direction that projects particles outward from the center of the Shape Transform.

Finally, Randomize Position moves the starting position by a random amount, up to the maximum value it contains.

Moving on to the four buttons at the bottom of the Shape Property, the first one can be clicked to toggle on or off the Shape gizmo editing mode. This acts in the same way as the Modify Collider button for colliders, allowing you to resize the boundaries or shape of the emitter volume in the Scene window.

The three other buttons allow you, respectively, to move, rotate, or scale the emitter volume, using guides such as arrows, which will appear in the Scene window as you toggle them.

The values in Velocity over Lifetime and Limit Velocity over Lifetime can be tweaked to make the particles gain or lose speed with time, respectively.

Inherit Velocity allows you to control the speed particles inherit from the emitter itself.

Force over Lifetime and Color over Lifetime contain properties that can be modified to make particles gain/lose force and exhibit color changes with time, respectively.

Color by Speed works in a way similar to Color over Lifetime but acts as per the speed of particles, rather than with time. Size and Rotation over/by Lifetime or Speed act similarly.

External Forces can be modified to make particles be affected by wind, for example. Noise lets you add turbulence to the movement of particles, and Collision lets you specify multiple collision planes that particles can collide with.

Triggers allow you to execute script code, based on whether particles are inside or outside collision shapes. Sub Emitters allow each particle to emit particles in another system. Texture Sheet Animation allows you to specify a texture sheet asset and animate/randomize it per particle. Lights lets you control light sources attached to particles, and Trails lets you attach trails to particles (which you will learn more about in the next section, "Trail Renderer"). Custom Date is quite complex and allows particles to interact with scripts or shaders.

As for the properties of Renderer, well, you can define how particles are rendered, i.e., control their color, trails, rendering mode, sorting mode, minimum/maximum size, alignment with respect to the camera, flip/pivot along axes, and how they interact with shadows/lights.

3.2.9 Trail Renderer

Trails are another form of Particle System that draw where a GameObject has been (Figure 3-29). Think of them as being tails. If you had a plane, for example, you might want it to have trails along its wings, to simulate the effect of flying through the air.

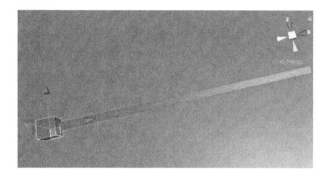

Figure 3-29. *A trail from a Trail Renderer component on a GameObject in the scene*

The first thing on a Trail Renderer (Figure 3-30) component is some sort of graph of Width (y axis) vs. Time (x axis). You can add more points on that graph, to make a trail bigger or smaller with time.

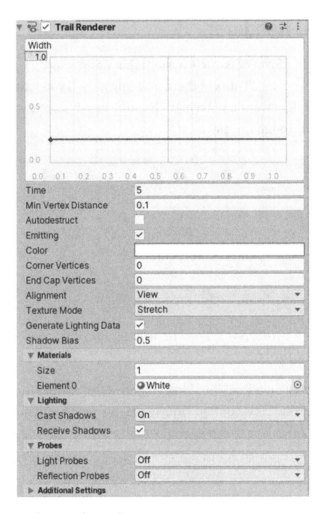

Figure 3-30. *The Trail Renderer component*

- The values of the Time axis (x axis) actually correspond to a percentage of the total time the trail has been set to render, as defined by the Time property (in our case, 5). This time value of 5 can be interpreted as the maximum time that the trail will persist. Following is an example. If the value is set to 10, and a car is continuously being driven, pieces of the trail will continuously be spawned, which will appear as if the trail will reach a maximum length value of 10. The trail will remain this long (appearing like a long rectangle), because new pieces are being spawned to replace the previous one from the car, at a maximum value of 10, until the car brakes. The trail will then become shorter and shorter, until it has a length of 0. This will take 10 seconds to occur, because each piece will be destroyed 10 seconds after it has been spawned, with the farthest pieces being the ones to disappear first.

- The values of the Width axis (y axis) will correspond to the width of the trail formed at a particular point in time.

Min Vertex Distance is the minimum distance at which to spawn from the previous one a new point on the trail.

Ticking Autodestruct automatically destroys the GameObject having that Trail Renderer as component when there is no trail. Unticking Emitting will pause trail generation.

Color allows you to set a gradient for the color along the trail. Corner Vertices is the amount of vertices to add for each corner. End Cap Vertices is the number of vertices to add at each end of the trail.

Alignment lets you rotate trails to face their transform component or the camera. If you choose to use the TransformZ mode, lines will be extruded along the XY plane of the Transform.

Texture mode, on the other hand, can be set to another mode, depending on how you want coordinates to be placed.

If ticked, Generate Lighting Data will generate data for shaders associated.

A Shadow Bias can be applied to prevent self-shadowing artifacts. A value of 0.5 represents 50% of the trail width at each segment.

You'll learn about materials in the next section, but for now, just assume that they define the color of the trail.

Lighting lets you choose how shadows are cast or received. Similarly, Probes, are about lighting and reflections.

3.3 Materials

As was previously discussed, materials can change the appearance of GameObjects equipped with a Renderer component. This includes the texture, color, and smoothness of an object, in addition to several other properties. The properties that a material possesses are defined by the shader that that material uses. A shader defines how an object looks, and a material can be thought of to be an instance of a shader, just like data types and variables. A material can be created in the Project window by right-clicking anywhere and heading to Create ➤ Material (Figure 3-31). You can rename the material just created.

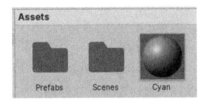

Figure 3-31. *Creating a material*

To apply a material to a GameObject in the scene, you can simply drag and drop it on the object in the Scene window directly, on the name of the GameObject in the Hierarchy window, or at the bottom of the Inspector view, if the GameObject in question is selected (Figure 3-32).

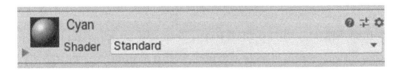

Figure 3-32. *Applying a material to a GameObject with a Renderer*

To edit properties of a material, you can simply expand it on any GameObject it has been applied to its renderer of, or select it in the Project window, doing so in the Inspector window (Figure 3-33).

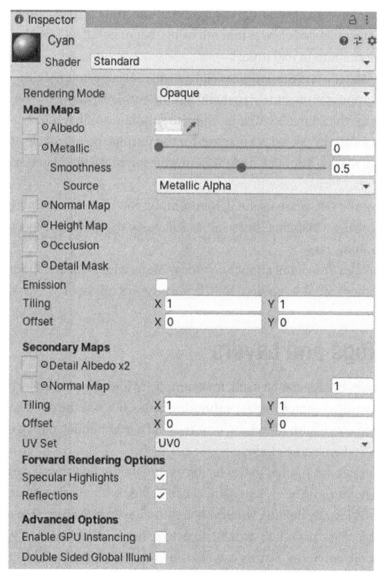

Figure 3-33. *Properties of a material*

By default, a created material will use the Standard Shader. This can be changed, matching specific requirements. The little transparent squares that appear beside properties can be assigned 2D textures, so that they don't appear plain, as they are by default.

Albedo is the main color of the material, and you can pick another color. All instances of objects that are using that material will display and apply the changes in real time.

The Metallic and Smoothness sliders will make the color of the material appear more or less metallic and smooth, respectively. You can also change the source to Albedo Alpha to simulate another effect.

As stated, you can set 2D textures for the normal, height, occlusion, and detail masks. After ticking Emission, you can make the material emit HDR colors.

Tiling and Offset are useful if, for example, you have a material using a grid 2D texture. Changing these values will make the material repeat itself or move along axes.

I won't go into detail about Secondary Maps and the other options, because these are not required for the purposes of this book.

3.4 Tags and Layers

As mentioned, tags can be used, for example, to identify what object collided with an enemy during a shooting game. If it was the player, we should remove health from him; otherwise, if it was a bullet, damage should be taken by the enemy.

Layers can be applied to GameObjects too. In the Editor, you can define whether a layer of GameObject can collide with another layer of GameObject. By default, when you create a Layer and assign it to a GameObject, it can collide with all objects, using existing Layers, if you don't modify anything. Layers can also be used to define what objects are rendered by the camera or affected by a particular light source.

In Edit ➤ Project Settings ➤ Physics, you can set many default physics properties, such as the value of Gravity and friction settings. We will be keeping everything as it is for now, but you can always change values, to better understand the changes on your own. Scrolling down, you will find the Layer Collision Matrix, with which you can set whether Layers of GameObjects can collide with those of other GameObjects (Figure 3-34). Note that unticking or disabling collision between two layers will make collision impossible between two GameObjects. Each of one of these two layers, including IsTrigger, calls what won't work anymore.

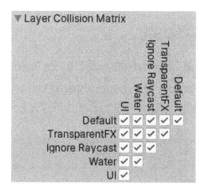

Figure 3-34. *An example of a Layer Collision matrix*

To create new Tags or Layers, head to Edit ➤ Project Settings ➤ Tags and Layers and expand the respective tabs. For tags, click the plus icon, enter a name, save, and close the window. For layers, type in the first empty rectangle you see named User Layer <num> and close the window (Figure 3-35).

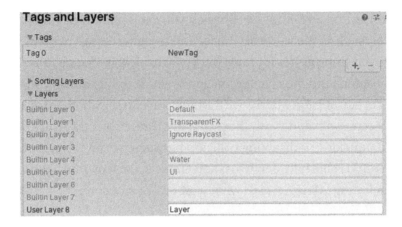

Figure 3-35. *Tags and layers*

To apply a tag or/and layer to a GameObject, select it in your Scene or Hierarchy window and select the respective tag or/and layer you want to apply to it (Figure 3-36).

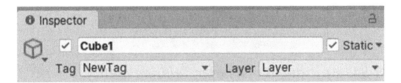

Figure 3-36. *Applying tags and layers to GameObjects*

3.5 Scripts

Scripts can be classified as both being a component and an actual independent asset. Scripts can only be written in UnityScript (like C#, with some modifications), as all other former languages have been deprecated. You can create scripts by either using the Add Component menu found at the bottom of the Inspector window when you select GameObject(s) and type the name of the script you wish to add, or right-click in the Project window and create one (Figure 3-37). Note that when you use the former option, and the script name you typed doesn't exist, you have the ability to directly create one.

Figure 3-37. *Creating scripts*

When a script has been created, you'll also be able to see it in your
Project window. Selecting a script displays a preview of its contents in the
Inspector (Figure 3-38).

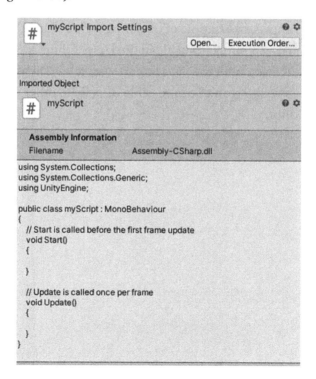

Figure 3-38. *Viewing scripts in the Inspector*

If you double-click the script, it will be opened in the code editor you set in Edit ➤ Preferences. The first three lines of any new script created serve to reference namespaces that contain classes. These will allow you to write code that makes use of popular and important data types, such as lists and arrays. The `using UnityEngine;` line will let you interact easily with other components in the engine, via your scripts.

Code you write in a script is normally placed between its starting and closing curly brackets. The `: MonoBehaviour` part is what's going to make your script actually behave like a component in Unity.

Next, if you want to declare global variables, you can do so outside any functions, within the curly brackets of the class.

Code written in the `void Start() {}` function will run once when you enter Play Mode. That written in `void Update() {}` will be executed once per frame. If your game is running at 60 FPS, the code in the update function will run 60 times in a second.

Figure 3-39 shows an example of declaring a global integer-type variable and making it publicly visible in the Unity Editor and to other scripts. Note that if you omit the `public` part, variables will by default be marked as `private` and won't be accessible directly to other scripts or visible in the Editor.

```
C# myScript.cs ×

Assets > C# myScript.cs > ⚡ myScript
    using System.Collections;
    using System.Collections.Generic;
    using UnityEngine;


    0 references
    public class myScript : MonoBehaviour
    {
        0 references
   💡   public int myInt;

        // Start is called before the first frame update
        0 references
        void Start()
        {

        }

        // Update is called once per frame
        0 references
        void Update()
        {

        }
    }
```

Figure 3-39. *How a script is by default + a global integer variable:*
myInt

After saving your script, and after it has been automatically compiled
in Unity, you should be able to see a new field on the GameObject that
has that script as component. Editing the value in that field in the Editor
directly changes the value that the myInt variable holds (Figure 3-40).
You'll learn more about scripting in Unity in later chapters.

▼ # ✓ **My Script (Script)**   ❷ ⇄ ⋮

Script   ⊕ myScript   ⊙
My Int   0

Figure 3-40. *Viewing and modifying script variables from the Inspector*

CHAPTER 4

User Interface

Typically, a user interface (UI) refers to the means by which a user interacts with a computer system. In our case, the term refers mostly to UI elements in our game, such as buttons and joysticks, which allow a player to interact with our game. In addition, this chapter will also discuss other types of UI elements, such as Text, Slider, and Image, which the player can't interact with but can be used to display important information or provide a better user experience. For this chapter, it is recommended that you use a 2D view. You can do so by clicking the little button labeled 2D at the top of the Scene window (Figure 4-1). Also, we'll be using the Rect tool (Figure 4-2).

Figures 4-1 and 4-2. *The 2D view button (left) and the Rect tool (right)*

© Kishan Takoordyal 2020
K. Takoordyal, *Beginning Unity Android Game Development*,
https://doi.org/10.1007/978-1-4842-6002-9_4

4.1 Canvas

In Unity, 2D UI elements must be the child of a GameObject known as Canvas. By default, whenever you create a UI element in the Editor, Unity will create the canvas and make the element a child of the latter, if no canvas has already been created. For now, let's look at the multiple components on an empty Canvas GameObject. This can be created by right-clicking in the Hierarchy window and selecting Canvas from the UI. You may also have noticed that another GameObject named EventSystem has been created in the scene. I will first analyze the different components found on the Canvas GameObject. If you zoom out in your scene view, the canvas should look like the following screenshot. Note that you can also double-click UI elements, or any GameObject for that matter, to bring them entirely in view (Figure 4-3).

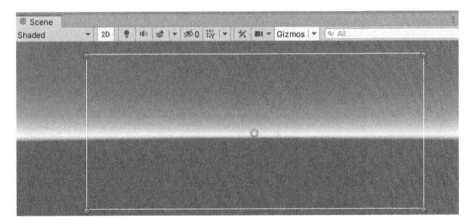

Figure 4-3. *The canvas as it appears in the Scene window in 2D view*

As just stated, UI elements need to be children of a Canvas GameObject in order to be visible and/or interactable. However, if, for example, a canvas has four UI elements of the same size as children and is found at the same exact position, the first elements will be drawn first on the screen, and the last ones will be drawn on top of them (demonstrated in section 4.3, "Text").

4.1.1 Canvas Component

There are three modes of rendering elements in the Canvas component (Figure 4-4).

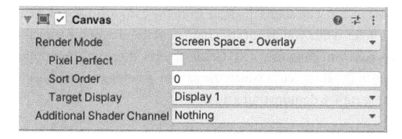

Figure 4-4. *The Canvas component*

In the first and default mode, Screen Space—Overlay, the canvas will be the size of the screen and, thus, match the latter's resolution. If Pixel Perfect is ticked, the UI will be rendered without anti-aliasing for precision. If multiple Canvas components with that same mode are used in the scene, the one with the highest Sort Order value will be the one that will be rendered. Changing the Target Display allows you to test multiple canvases, or views, in the Editor. I won't really go into great detail about that option or about the Additional Shader Channel.

If the mode is set to Screen Space—Camera (Figure 4-5), the canvas and its child elements will be rendered with respect to the Camera GameObject assigned.

Render Mode	Screen Space - Camera	▼
Pixel Perfect	☐	
Render Camera	▥◄ Main Camera (Camera)	⊙
Plane Distance	0	
Sorting Layer	Default	▼

Figure 4-5. *The Canvas component set to a Screen Space—Camera Render Mode*

Another way of saying this is that the canvas can be thought to then act as a plane. You can set its distance from the camera in the Plane Distance field. While you won't see changes in the size of the canvas if, for example, you're making use of 3D GameObjects, there will be a noticeable difference in the distance at which the canvas is being rendered from the camera. Figure 4-6 demonstrates this.

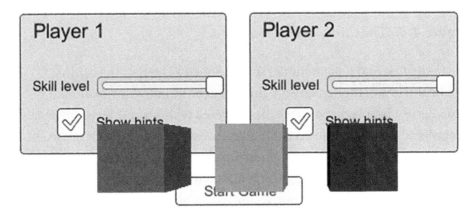

Figure 4-6. *An example of a canvas with a Camera Screen Space mode and 3D objects*

The third and final mode, World Canvas, makes the canvas behave as a 3D plane in the game. Using this mode allows you to have as many Canvas GameObjects in a scene as you want, and they will all be rendered by the camera assigned. For example, in a game, this mode can be used to make floating health bars over enemies. The canvas would thus be at the same 3D position and rotation as the enemy its child slider represents the health of. Figure 4-7 illustrates an example.

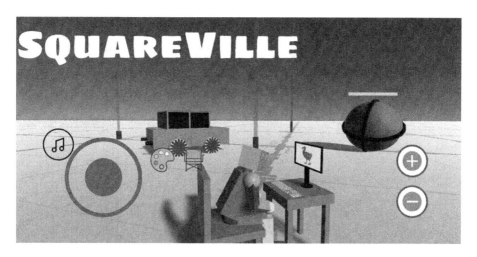

Figure 4-7. *A canvas with a health bar in World Space*

The screen of the monitor also makes use of a World Space Canvas GameObject.

4.1.2 Canvas Scaler

The Canvas Scaler (Figure 4-8) is a very useful component that allows us to specify how our canvas(es) should be rendered with respect to different screen sizes. It works only with the Screen Space modes of the previous component.

▼ 🔲 ✓ Canvas Scaler		❷ ⇄ ⋮
UI Scale Mode	Constant Pixel Size	▼
Scale Factor	1	
Reference Pixels Per Unit	100	

Figure 4-8. *The Canvas Scaler component*

In the first mode, the canvas will always be the same size. If, for example, you make a game for a 720p screen and accordingly resize your elements to match this, when that resolution is doubled, all elements will still be of the same physical size and, thus, appear two times smaller, provided the screen size is constant for both the 720p and 1440p screen (Figure 4-9). Increasing the Scale Factor will make the canvas proportionally bigger. The last option applies to Sprites, which we won't make use of, because we are more concerned with 2D games.

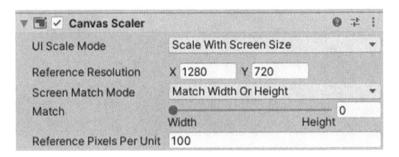

Figure 4-9. *The Canvas Scaler component set to scale with screen size*

You can set a reference resolution for which you're targeting the game to be developed for. Then, you can choose from making the canvas match the screen width or height, or shrink, or expand accordingly. For the former, you can set a canvas to match only the width or height of the screen. Bringing the slider all the way to the left, for example, will make the canvas indifferent, whether the height in pixels of a screen size is increased or not, while width is kept constant. However, in that case, if the width of a screen in pixels is changed, the canvas will scale in equal proportions.

Finally, in the last mode, Constant Physical Size, you can set the actual physical size of the canvas in terms of centimeters, millimeters, inches, points, or picas. That's really all you need to know about that.

As this book aims to help you develop mobile games, specifically for the Android platform, the Canvas Scaler usually is set to match the height, if we're creating a game in landscape. For example, if we have a phone that has a 1920 × 1080 resolution, and the game will play in landscape (horizontally), the final screen height will correspond to the value 1080. Commonly, screens become larger vertically rather than horizontally. Our statement attempts to convey that if we have phones with aspect ratios of 16:9, 18:9, or 21:9, for example, our buttons and other elements will remain of the same size, unless the screen is actually larger rather than longer. Our game will thus be able to play full-screen on these devices, without affecting how our elements are laid out, such as in terms of their scale. Now, if our game was played on a device with a larger screen, not only a longer one, it would scale and still display properly. Depending on the game you're trying to make, this won't always be what you're wishing to do, and you might pursue another option.

4.1.3 Graphic Raycaster

This component (Figure 4-10) is basically used to determine whether an element on the canvas has been hit or not.

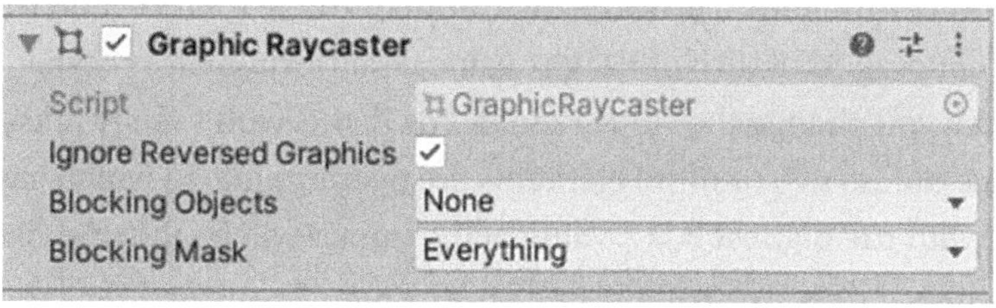

Figure 4-10. *The Graphic Raycaster component*

I won't go into detail about the properties, because you'll rarely interact with this component. Just so you know, they are used for tweaking what object(s) should be able to block the raycast.

4.2 Rect Transform

This is a component that you'll see on all UI-type GameObjects (Figure 4-11). It is the equivalent of the Transform component on 3D GameObjects but for UI elements, with some additional options and properties. For the Canvas GameObject, values in this component might be locked.

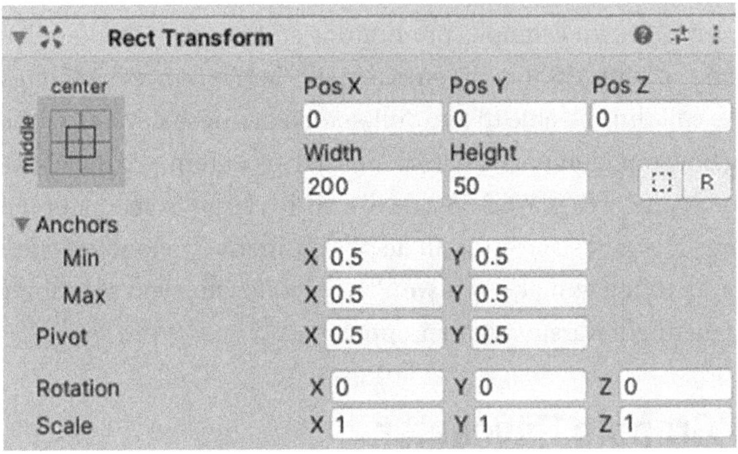

Figure 4-11. *The Rect Transform component*

The Pos X, Y, and Z correspond to the typical position Vector3 of a Transform component. The same logic applies to the rotation and scale fields. Changing the Width or Height value is self-explanatory. Take note that if you change the value held in Pos Z, this won't really make a difference unless two or more elements are overlapping, in which case the element with the highest Pos Z value of the bunch will be the one visible. For example, if there were many empty 2D squares (Images), each having the same size and found exactly at the same position but each having a different color, the one with the highest Pos Z of the group would be the one visible. There are exceptions to this rule, however. Note, too, that the name and number of fields will differ, based on the selected Anchor type.

Anchors designate the point where the position of the UI element should be relative to their parent's Rect Transform and position. Each of the Min and Max values can be in the range of 0 to 1 in terms in X and Y coordinate axes. An X value of 0 corresponds to the leftmost position of the canvas while one of 1 corresponds to the rightmost. Similarly, this range goes from the uppermost position of the canvas to the bottommost for the Y value. Usually the Vector2 Min and Max values are the same.

While Anchors had to do with the positioning of the element relative to their parents itself, the Pivot is all about moving the center of the UI element relative to itself. Again, X and Y values go from 0 to 1, but this time, these represent the positioning of something known as the pivot of the UI element based on its own width and height. For example, if the X pivot value was set to 0 and you'd try to increase the width of the element, the pivot would be at the leftmost end, and the element would scale only from its right side unlike it would from its center in both horizontal directions if that value was 0.5, i.e., at the center of the element.

You can also visually change the Anchor points and pivot of an element by clicking the grid-looking thing at the top-left corner of a Rect Transform component (Figure 4-12).

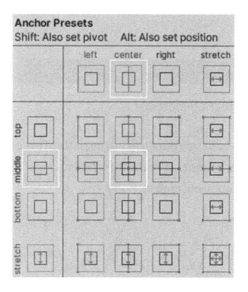

Figure 4-12. *Anchor Presets*

Clicking any of these presets will automatically assign its anchor values to the element. Additionally, if the Shift button is also held while doing so, the pivot value will also get modified in a similar fashion. If the Alt button is held in the process, independent of whether the Shift one is held or not, the element will also move to that anchor position and thus have a `Vector2` position of (0, 0). You'll be able to test all these after you've learned about other Canvas UI elements.

4.3 Text

To create a UI element, simply right-click in an empty space in the Hierarchy window, head to UI, and choose the element you require. For this section, we'll be looking at the UI element named Text. Make sure it is a child of a Canvas GameObject. Double left-clicking the element should make it visible and centered in your Scene window (Figure 4-13).

Figure 4-13. *The Text UI element*

Of course, you can drag along the edges of the Text element, to make it occupy a bigger area, or manually modify the values of its Rect Transform component, for that matter (Figure 4-14).

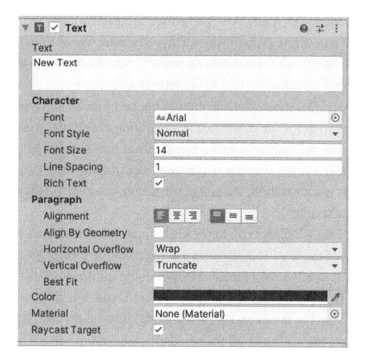

Figure 4-14. *The Text component*

Modifying the field where "New Text" is written by default on a Text component directly changes what's actually written on the element.

Next, you can specify the font to be used, if you imported font files in your Project. You can choose from normal, bold, and/or italic font styles for your Text element, as well as specify the font size and line spacing. For example, a larger font size value will make text appear bigger, and a smaller value of line spacing will reduce the distance between lines in a paragraph. Ticking Rich Text allows you to style specific words in your text, such as by placing them between HTML-like tags.

Further on, you can align your text at the left, center, or right and at the top, center, or bottom of the area its Rect Transform component occupies. Ticking Align By Geometry will execute some minor changes to make the text reflect more of your previous choice, in terms of its actual geometry.

For Horizontal Overflow, you can either choose to make the text continue on a new line (Wrap) when a line has more words than the width of the Rect Transform can hold or just ignore the width of the Rect Transform and continue on that same line (Overflow).

For Vertical Overflow, you can either choose Truncate or Overflow. In a similar fashion, in the latter, the text will continue ahead of the edge of the height of the Rect Transform and occupy only as much space as it requires, whereas in the former, after the maximum lines that the Rect Transform can hold has been reached, the rest of the text or lines will be discarded and won't be visible.

Ticking Best Fit allows you to set a minimum and maximum size for the font size of the text. These values will override the former Font Size field. The text won't have a font size less than the minimum value and will tend to have a font size as close as possible to the maximum value, as long as the Rect Transform has an area sufficient to hold all the text. If the Rect Transform can easily house all the text at that minimum value, Font Size will internally be incremented to a higher value, but less or equal to that maximum value set while the Rect Transform can hold the full text.

Note that if you specify a font size or a minimum font size in Best Fit larger than what the Rect Transform can hold while not using overflow modes, some or all the characters in the text might not be visible.

Next, you can change the color of the text and assign a material, if you want your text to have some effect, such as a horizontal gradient.

Ticking Raycast Target allows you to add events later via script when, for example, you want something to occur when the Text UI element is clicked.

4.4 Image

Remember that UI elements that are at the bottom of the list of the children of the Canvas get rendered on top of the ones that are above them in that list? Well, here's what happens if we create a UI Image element and place it before a Text element in the list of Canvas children (Figure 4-15):

Figure 4-15. *Rendering an Image over a Text UI element*

If, however, the Text and Image elements switch places, the Image will be in front or on top of the Text element (Figure 4-16).

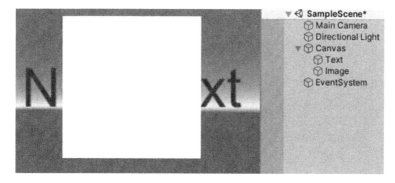

Figure 4-16. *Rendering a Text over an Image UI element*

This component can be used to display a noninteractive image to the user. You can use this for such elements as decorations or icons (Figure 4-17).

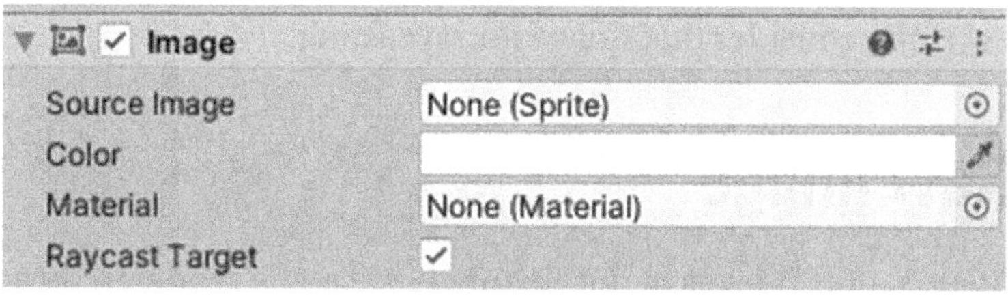

Figure 4-17. *The Image component*

117

Image can be set to display an actual picture graphic. Note that the image will be scaled to match the dimensions of the Rect Transform. You can mark an Image asset to be a Sprite 2D type, so that you can assign it to the Source Image property of a UI Image component, so that it displays that image. To mark an imported image as a Sprite 2D type, you just have to select it in the Project window and change its Texture Type to Sprite (2D and UI) in the Inspector (Figure 4-18). In Chapter 6, we'll be using a Sprite 2D texture for a Pause button.

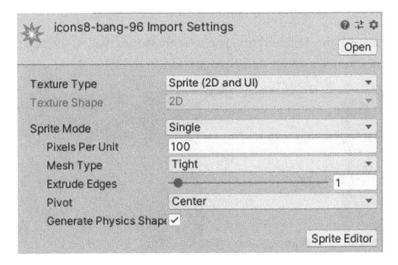

Figure 4-18. *A texture marked as Sprite 2D*

Setting another color on the Image Component can be thought of as putting a color filter on an image. The Material property can be used to apply other effects on the final image to be rendered. Ticking Raycast Target lets Unity consider that image for raycasting.

4.5 Raw Image

Unlike Images, only images of the Texture type can be rendered on a Raw Image component (Figure 4-19).

▼ 🖾 ✓ **Raw Image**		❷ ⇄ ⋮
Texture	None (Texture)	⊙
Color		🖋
Material	None (Material)	⊙
Raycast Target	✓	
UV Rect	X 0	Y 0
	W 1	H 1

Figure 4-19. *The Raw Image component*

The Color and Material properties work similarly to those in Image components. As for the Vector2 values X and Y and W and H, they correspond, respectively, to the positioning and size of the Texture assigned, relative to the Rect Transform component. Modifying the X and Y values will make the Texture offset by X and Y amounts from the center of the Rect Transform, and modifying the W and H values will, accordingly, change the width and height of the Texture with respect to the actual width and height of the Rect Transform.

4.6 Slider

The Slider UI element can be useful in various situations. They can be used to make health bars for enemies and/or the player easily, or be interactable, in order to change some in-game value, such as volume (Figures 4-20 and 4-21).

Figure 4-20. *A slider*

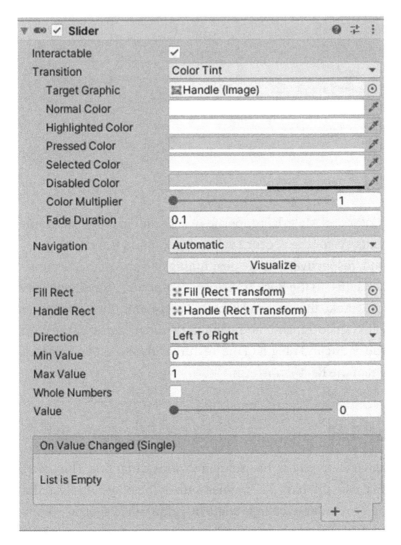

Figure 4-21. *The Slider component*

If Interactable is kept ticked, you will be able to drag and adjust the slider's knob when the game is played. Transition allows you to set visual feedback, depending on the value of the slider or the state of the knob.

For example, using a Color Tint transition allows you to set defined colors for the knob, depending on whether it is disabled or pressed. In a similar fashion, Sprite Swap causes a defined change in the Sprite that is being used, and Animation will accordingly trigger set animations. Of course, there will be no change if the Transition has been set to None.

The options in Navigation allow you to control the slider via keyboard keys. If you don't want a slider's value to change, using the keyboard keys, set this property to None. Fill Rect and Handle Rect are Rect Transform components that must be assigned, in order for the slider to know where its Fill and Handle are found.

Direction defines visually where the min and max values of the slider are found. If this is set to Right to Left, the smallest value the slider can hold will be found visually at the far-right end of the slider.

Just below the Direction property, there are two fields that allow you to set the minimum and maximum values that the slider can hold. If the Knob is found at either end of the slider, it will either represent the minimum or maximum values set in the fields I just discussed, depending on the Direction property.

Ticking Whole Number will ensure that values the slider represents will be integers only. Numbers with a decimal/fractional part won't occur while this is kept ticked.

Changes made by adjusting the Value slider will also be reflected by the slider in the Scene and Game Windows. This Value slider goes all the way from the minimum value (left) set to the maximum value (right) set.

Finally, you can set the slider to do something whenever its value is changed. For example, you can make the slider call a function in some script on a GameObject when its value is changed. We will make use of this later.

Next, let's take a quick look at the children that form part of a Slider GameObject by default (Figure 4-22).

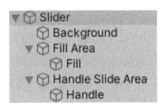

Figure 4-22. *The children GameObjects of a typical Slider UI element*

Background has an Image component and is of the full size of a Slider GameObject. Changing properties of that component will directly alter the background of the slider.

The Fill Area is just an empty GameObject, but it is required in order for the fill of the slider to work properly. Next, Fill GameObject works similarly to Background GameObject. As the slider has a value closer to its maximum value, the fill will occupy a larger area and cover the background.

Handle Fill Area denotes the area in which the Handle of a slider can move. Finally, the Handle is just an Image Component (with a Rect Transform) that uses a plain white Circle sprite by default. The handle is the visual component you'll interact with, if you decide to change the value of a slider in-game.

4.7 Button

Button can be thought of as that clicky component that you interact with in a game in order to do something. A good example of a button could be something that looks like an arrow that makes your character jump when you press it. By default, a button looks like the following when created (Figure 4-23):

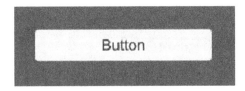

Figure 4-23. *A button*

To change the size of a button, just edit the appropriate values in the Rect Transform component of its GameObject. To change its default looks, edit the Image component on its GameObject, as desired (Figure 4-24).

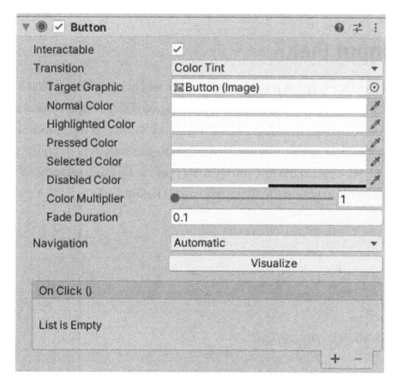

Figure 4-24. *The Button component*

The first couple of properties do the same thing as those of a Slider component. You won't be able to interact with a button if Interactable is not ticked. Transition basically defines how the button should look, depending on states such as when it is pressed or disabled.

A smaller value of Fade Duration will reflect changes made quicker. For example, if the button is pressed, and a Color Tint transition is being used, the button will instantly transition to a color specified in Pressed Color, if the Fade Duration value is set to 0 (seconds).

Again, the button can be set to perform certain actions, as defined in the OnClick() list at the bottom of that component.

By default, a button also has a Text GameObject as a child. You can safely delete or destroy it, if you don't need it, however.

4.8 Input Field

An Input Field is really just a text box. Clicking it will bring up the default keyboard on a mobile device and allow you the possibility of typing something. As children, it has two Text UI elements. The first is known as the Placeholder and will contain some dummy text while nothing has been typed. The other Text UI element will contain the text you type. You can modify the properties of these Text UI elements to obtain the styling you want (Figure 4-25).

Figure 4-25. *An input field*

On an Input Field component, you will again find the Interactable, Transition, and Navigation properties. These will do the same things as in Button and Slider.

The properties related to Text represent, respectively, the Text UI element to use to display typed content, a field directly mapped to the text property of that Text UI element, and the maximum number of characters that that Input Field can hold. Note that the Placeholder text will disappear, unless there is nothing set in the Text property. If this is not blank, the data entered by the user will already be preceded by the text we set.

Choosing a proper Content Type for the type of data to be entered is useful to define how data entered will be displayed (Figure 4-26).

For example, if set to Password, when a user enters something in the Input Field, all characters will automatically be replaced by asterisks. Visit the documentation for InputField to learn the difference between the many Content Type options.

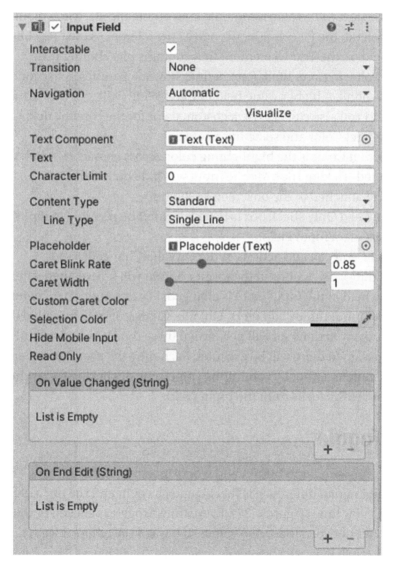

Figure 4-26. *The Input Field component*

Depending on the value you set in Content Type, you might also have a Line Type property, which allows you to choose whether data can be formatted only in a single line (Single Line), whether it can be formatted across multiple lines, or if the user can span a new line by pressing the Enter/Return key (Multi Line Newline) or not (Multi Line Submit). With the latter option, the text will go across multiple lines automatically, when required.

By default, the Placeholder property only references the first child of an Input Field, as the Text UI element that contains placeholder text.

The value in Caret Blink Rate defines how many times per second the caret will blink. A higher value held in Caret Width will make the caret wider, and you also can choose a custom color for the caret by ticking the Custom Caret Color and selecting a color.

Selection Color is the highlighting color across characters when they are selected. Ticking Hide Mobile Input will hide on iOS devices the native input field attached to the onscreen keyboard.

If the Read Only check box is ticked, it won't be possible to input more characters in an Input Field.

Finally, you can add actions to the OnValueChanged() and OnEndEdit() lists. Actions in the former option will be executed whenever the value held in the Input Field is changed. For example, if you enter Play mode and input three characters, OnValueChanged() will be called three times, and any actions set will performed three times. As for OnEndEdit(), actions assigned there will be executed each time the user finishes editing the text content, either by submitting something or clicking somewhere that removes the focus from the Input Field.

4.9 Toggle

Toggle is very similar to Button and works mostly in the same way. The only fundamental difference is that Toggle has either a True or False value at a particular time (Figure 4-27). Every time a toggle is clicked or touched, it alternates between these two values. If it was True before it was clicked/touched, it will have a False value; otherwise, it will have a True value.

Figure 4-27. *A toggle*

On a Toggle Component (Figure 4-28), IsOn denotes the True/False state of the Toggle UI element. While this is ticked, the Toggle is in a True state.

The Toggle Transition property allows you to set a visual effect for when a user interacts with the Toggle UI element.

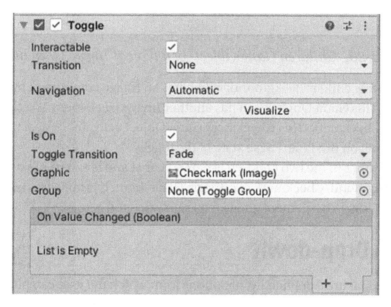

Figure 4-28. *The Toggle component*

Graphic is set to a GameObject having an Image component. This Graphic will represent the True/False state of the Toggle UI element.

127

As for the Group property, you can assign a GameObject having a Toggle Group component here. A toggle group is basically a collection of Toggle UI elements. It can be useful sometimes to have only one toggle in many to have a True state at a time, for example. This is exactly why toggle groups might come in handy, but they are outside the scope of this book.

And as with most of the previous UI elements introduced, some action(s) can be executed when the value of the toggle has been changed.

A Toggle GameObject has two children by default (Figure 4-29).

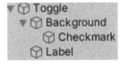

Figure 4-29. *Children GameObjects of a typical Toggle UI element*

The first child is Background, which has an Image component by default. This GameObject itself has another Image UI element as a child, named Checkmark. This Checkmark GameObject activates or deactivates, depending on the True/False state of the toggle.

The other of the two children is named Label and is just the Text beside the Background/Checkmark of a Toggle UI element. It is not a fundamental part of a Toggle UI element and can be safely deleted.

4.10 Drop-down

Imagine making a defined list of options from which the user can pick one. This is exactly why the Dropdown UI element exists in Unity (Figure 4-30).

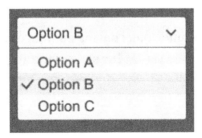

Figure 4-30. *A drop-down menu*

When a drop-down is touched/clicked, an expanded menu with all predefined options is displayed. If the number of options requires a bigger area to be displayed than what's already defined for the drop-down, a scrollbar will be displayed on the right side of the list of options. After an option has been selected, the drop-down will collapse back to its initial state, displaying the currently selected option.

A Dropdown UI element has a long list of children, but because of their precise names, and by using the Rect tool, you can easily understand the purposes they serve (Figure 4-31). In this section, we will examine only the new properties present in the Dropdown component.

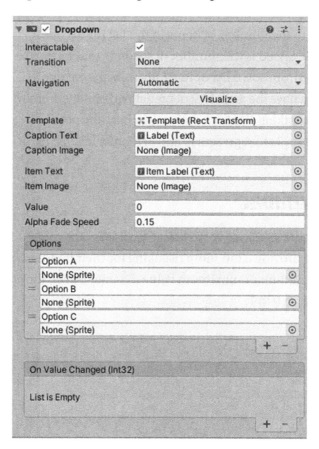

Figure 4-31. *The Dropdown component*

Template, Caption Text, and Caption Image are all references to Rect Transform, Text, and Image components, respectively. Template is by default the GameObject that contains many children, which all form part of the list that appears when a drop-down is clicked/touched. Caption Text denotes the Text component in which the name of the currently selected option will be written. Caption Image is not necessary but represents the Image Component that will feature the image representing the currently selected option.

Item Text and Item Image work in quite the same way as Caption Text and Caption Image but will, this time, represent options in the drop-down list generally.

Value is the index of the currently selected option in the list of options. It goes from 0 to the number of items in the list minus one.

Alpha Fade Speed is the number of seconds that it takes to transition to a fully opaque drop-down list or to a fully transparent one.

Finally, you have the actual list of predefined options, from which you can add or remove options. For each option, you have the possibility to change a name, assign a sprite to represent it, and to reorder it in the list of options.

4.11 Scrollbar

Scrollbars (Figure 4-32) are very similar to sliders. The main differences are that scrollbars provide a tad more tweaking for their handles, but instead of having a minimum or maximum value that can be set, they can only have a value from 0 to 1.

Figure 4-32. *A scrollbar*

The handle of a scrollbar will be positioned near its left edge, if the scrollbar has a value of 0, and near the right edge for a value of 1.

You can refer to the section about sliders to understand most of the properties provided by a Scrollbar component (Figure 4-33). The only two new properties are Size and Number of Steps.

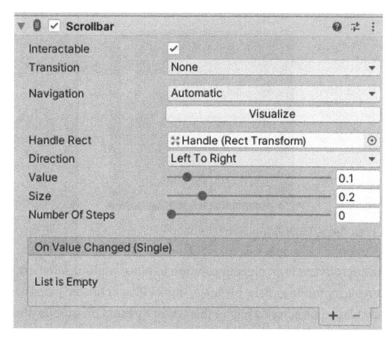

Figure 4-33. *The Scrollbar component*

The Size slider will always have a value between 0 and 1. A value of 1 will make the handle have a width and height equal to that of the Rect Transform component. Number of Steps will define the number of possible stops that the scrollbar will have while its handle is being dragged. For example, if that property gets set to a value of 4, when you enter the Play mode and drag on the slider, there will be only four positions along the whole width of the scrollbar where the handle can be positioned at a time. The default value of 0 allows the handle to be freely positioned anywhere along that width.

4.12 Scrollview

The Scrollview UI element has a viewport (Figure 4-34). In it, you can place several UI elements, such as Text, Image, or Button. It also comes with horizontal and vertical scrollbars by default. You can use these to scroll between the elements you place in its viewport.

Figure 4-34. *A scrollview*

Using a scrollview is an elegant solution to place multiple elements in a defined area for mobile games, because, unlike PC or console games, which are usually played on screens bigger than those present on mobile phones, mobile game developers regularly have to display multiple elements that can't often be made too small, as then the end user will find it difficult to interact with, or won't properly perceive, what's represented. A scrollview can also be used to scroll across a large Image or Text element too.

Content represents the Rect Transform of the child of the scrollview that will house all the elements that you place in its viewport (Figure 4-35).

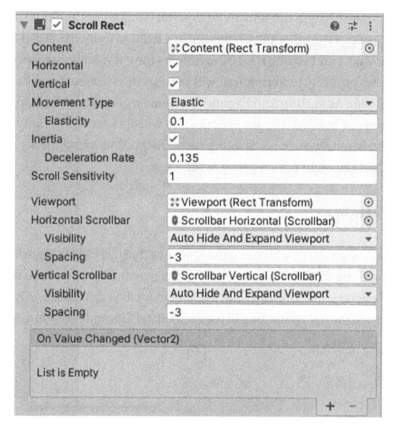

Figure 4-35. *The Scrollview component*

Not ticking Horizontal or Vertical will disable the respective scrollbar at runtime. The movement type can be set to either Unrestricted, Elastic, or Clamped. Using the two last options will make the content remain within the bounds of the Scroll Rect. Elastic will bounce the content when it reaches the edge of the Scroll Rect, however. The amount of bounce in the latter will be determined by the Elasticity property.

If Inertia is ticked, the content will continue to move when the handle is released after a drag. If not, the content will only move when dragged. If Inertia is set, the Deceleration Rate will determine how quickly the content will stop moving. A rate of 0 will stop the movement immediately, while a rate of 1 will make the movement never slow down.

Scroll sensitivity is the sensitivity to scroll using wheel and trackpad events. Some of the other properties are just used to point the Scroll Rect to the viewport and scrollbars. The scrollbars have a visibility property. Setting that property to Permanent will prevent the scrollbar from being hidden, while Auto Hide And Expand Viewport will make the content hide when not needed. The latter of the two will also cause the viewport to expand when that occurs. Spacing is the distance between the scrollbar and the bottom-right corner of the Scroll Rect.

4.13 Panel

A panel is just an image with some transparency that has its Rect Transform stretching along the full width and height of its parent. That is, if you make a Panel UI element the child of a Canvas element set to Screen Space—Overlay, it will occupy the full visible area of your screen in Play mode (Figure 4-36).

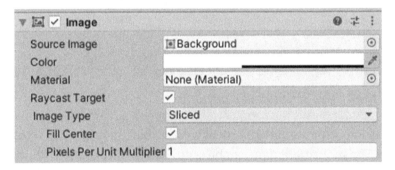

Figure 4-36. *The Panel component*

4.14 EventSystem

Event System is a component that controls all interactions with the UI system, receiving inputs from keyboard, mouse, touch screen, etc., and translating them to interactions with the underlying UI elements (Figure 4-37).

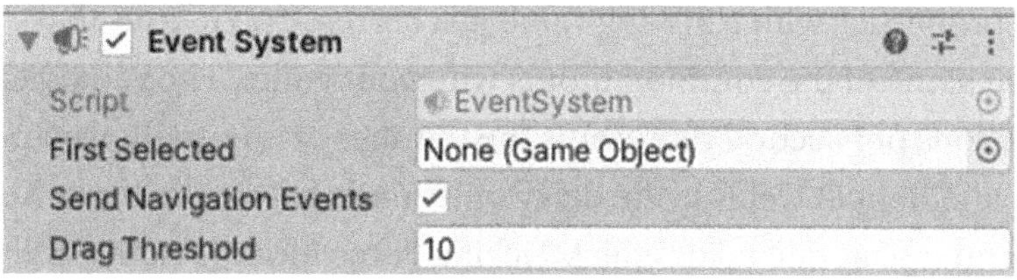

Figure 4-37. *The Event System component*

It works out which canvas and control the user has interacted with and activates it accordingly. Without Event System, the UI would merely draw on the screen and do nothing.

Additionally, Event System allows UI controls (which support events, such as check boxes and buttons) to inform the Unity project when the user has interacted with them. For example, a user clicks a button, the button then activates or deactivates another GameObject. This can be a very powerful system, if used correctly.

First Selected corresponds to the GameObject that was selected first at runtime. Ticking Send Navigation Events allows EventSystem to send navigation events, such as Move, Submit, and Cancel. Drag Threshold corresponds to the soft area for dragging in pixels.

The Standalone Input Module (Figure 4-38) is the component that actually detects input (keyboard key presses, mouse pointer clicks, touches) and sends the corresponding event to the game. Without this component, you wouldn't be able to interact with your game.

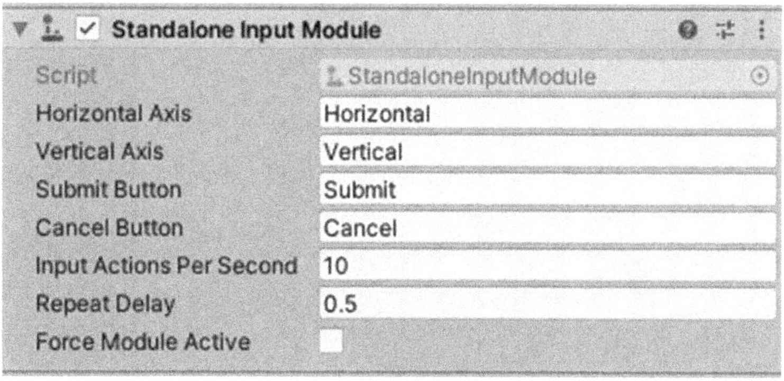

Figure 4-38. *The Standalone Input Module component*

The properties with a `String` value just correspond to axes that represent some of the common inputs with your game. The value held in Input Actions per second represents the number of inputs allowed per second, and Repeat Delay is the delay in seconds before the Input Actions per Second repeat rate takes effect. Ticking Force Module Active will force the Standalone Input Module to be active.

We won't have to edit any property of any of the components found on our Event System in the game we will be making.

4.15 Introduction to Input Axes

As we will be concentrating on making mobile games, it is important, for many types of games, to know how axes work. To interact with an adventure 3D mobile game, you might want to use a joystick, to move the player. This joystick will most probably make use of an axis or axes.

A joystick such as the following (Figure 4-39) can be used to move the player's character in all directions in a 3D game. The player can hold and move the handle of the joystick in the direction they prefer their character to go.

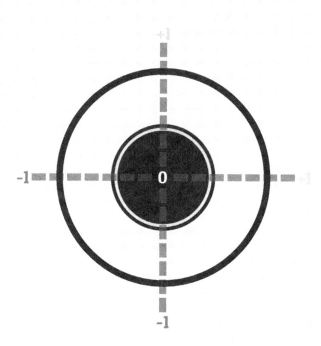

Figure 4-39. *Typical illustration of joystick axes*

That joystick shown makes use of two axes: a horizontal one and a vertical one. When the handle is not pressed, it sits in the middle of the total area of the joystick. At this position, it has a value of 0 for both its axes. Referring to the preceding figure, if the handle is pushed to the top-left corner, it will have an approximate value of -0.5 to represent its horizontal axis and another of +0.5 or 0.5 for its vertical axis.

You will soon learn to make use of joysticks in a mobile game and how to map them to actually trigger actions of the character. Another fun thing that joysticks allow us to do is to modify the speed of the character, based on the value of one of its axes. For example, if we set the maximum speed of our character to 10 units/second, we can multiply that by the current value of the vertical axis of our joystick, so that we can make our character go slower, by not fully pushing the joystick handle up.

137

CHAPTER 5

Building Our First Android Game: Sphere Shooter

That's it, we're now ready to build an actual 3D mobile game in Unity! In this chapter, we're going to make a simple game. Basically, our game character will be a cube with a turret (we'll be calling this a tank). Using two joysticks, a player can move the tank and fire bullets. Next, we're going to make an enemy and spawn copies of it. Enemies will try to go in the same direction as the player's tank, and the aim of the game will be to destroy them before they succeed.

5.1 Render Pipelines

The process of drawing graphics to the screen (or to a render texture) is known as rendering. This process is one of the key factors affecting performance in games. By default, the main camera in Unity renders its view to the screen.

Recently, Unity released the Scriptable Render Pipeline (SRP). An SRP aims to allow developers to control rendering via scripts, thus providing a high degree of customization.

Among the many possible Render Pipelines that can be created using SRP, Unity provided two prebuilt SRPs: the High Definition Render Pipeline (HDRP) and the Universal Render Pipeline (URP).

While HDRP lets you create cutting-edge, high-fidelity graphics for high-end platforms, we won't be using it for making mobile games, because it has a high performance cost.

5.1.1 Universal Render Pipeline (URP)

URP is a very elegant solution for making mobile games. It provides several graphics/quality options that can be tweaked very easily, and in many genres of games, it has been proven to provide a noticeable performance boost over the default Render Pipeline that Unity uses for making a new project.

You can make a new project that uses URP by default, but for the sake of explaining how to add it to an existing project, we'll choose instead the standard option (Figure 5-1).

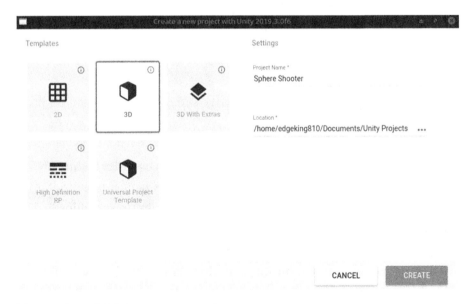

Figure 5-1. *Making a new project*

Primarily, I will be targeting the 1920 × 1080 resolution or the 16:9 aspect ratio for the game we'll be making (Figure 5-2).

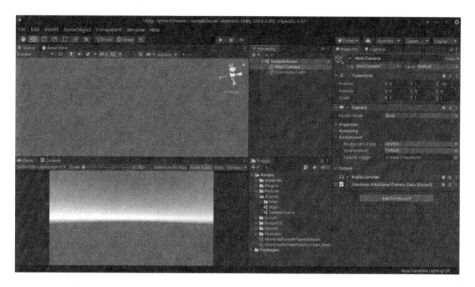

Figure 5-2. *The layout of my Editor*

Finally, for this section, we'll be adding the URP package to our game and switching our game project, to make use of it. Head over to Window ➤ Package Manager. You might have to wait a bit before the long list of packages is loaded. If that doesn't occur after everything seemingly has been loaded, click around in the Package Manager window.

Scroll or search for the Universal RP package. When that's done, click it. Hit install and wait for everything to be imported (Figure 5-3). You can close the Package Manager window once that's done, because we won't require any more packages from there.

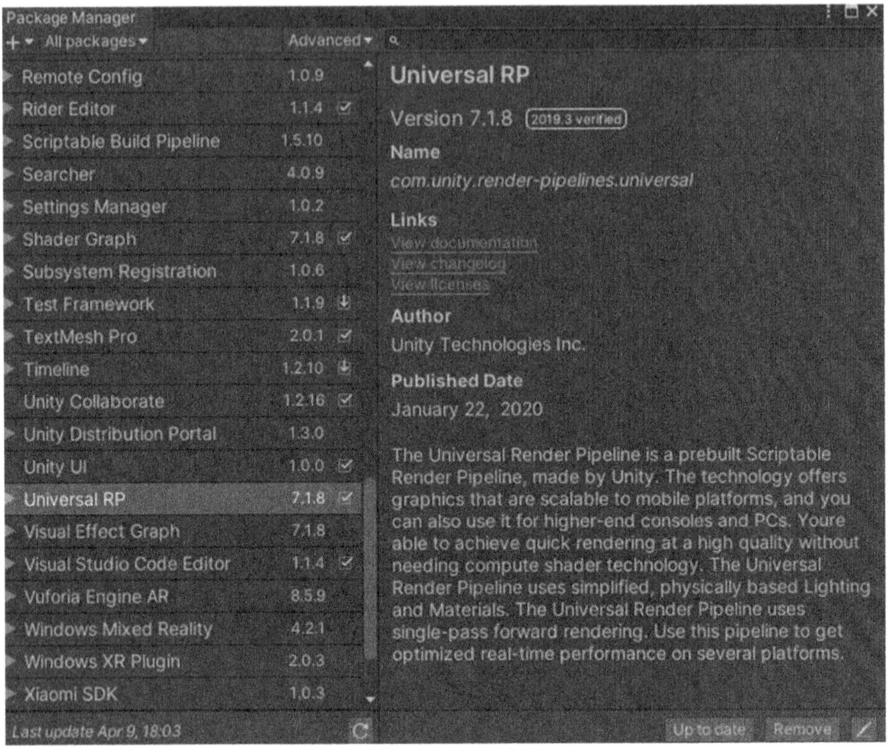

Figure 5-3. *Installing the Universal RP package from the Package Manager window*

Finally, to allow our project make use of URP, we must tell it to do so. First, right-click anywhere in your Project window and click Create ➤ Rendering ➤ Universal Render Pipeline ➤ Pipeline Asset (Forward Renderer). This will create an asset for URP with many properties that can be tweaked to easily change the graphics/quality of our game. Two new assets should appear in your project window (Figure 5-4).

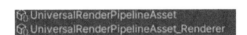

Figure 5-4. *URP Pipeline assets*

At this point, you must know what the different properties do. All we have left to do now is to drag and drop the URP Pipeline Asset we just created into the Scriptable Render Pipeline Settings tab (Figure 5-5) found in Edit ➤ Project Settings ➤ Graphics.

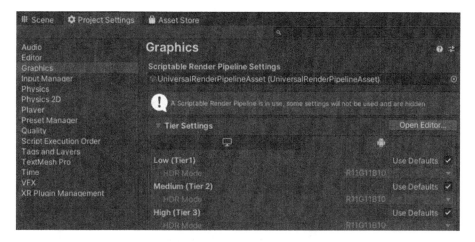

Figure 5-5. *Adding an SRP in the Graphics section of Project Settings*

One important thing to remember is that if you are working on a project, and you decide to switch its Render Pipeline, you must ensure that all the materials you are working with are using a shader compatible with the new Render Pipeline you want to use. Otherwise, everything in your Scene/Game windows will appear pink. Fortunately, Unity provides an easy solution.

If the new Render Pipeline you are switching to is URP (you'll have to do a similar thing for HDRP), in addition to everything I discussed previously in this section, you will have to click Edit ➤ Render Pipeline ➤ Universal Render Pipeline ➤ Upgrade Project Materials to UniversalRP Materials. Doing so will automatically upgrade all materials in your project to use the equivalent shader that URP provides. You can also choose the second option, which is to upgrade only the materials you select, depending on your needs.

To complete this section and start working on the fun part, just switch the build platform of the project to Android. Open the Build

Settings (Ctrl+Shift+B or File ➤ Build Settings), click the Android option, making sure it's highlighted, and hit Switch Platform (found near the bottom-left corner). A Unity logo should appear beside the Android label on its right, and you can close the Build Settings window (Figure 5-6). Often, if the step of switching to a different platform is done later in the development of a game, many assets, such as sprites or textures, will have to be done again, which takes quite a bit of time. That's why it's best to do switch platforms at an early stage in the creation of a game, if you're sure of what platform you're primarily focused on developing for.

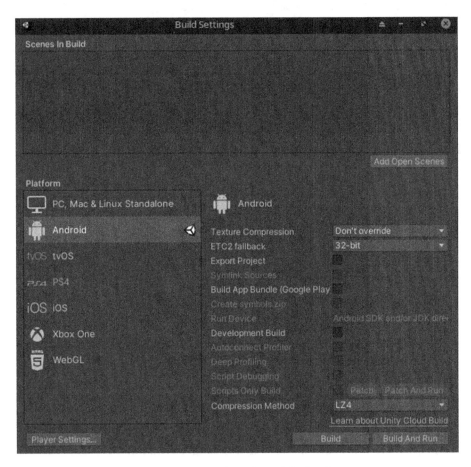

Figure 5-6. *Switching to the Android Build platform*

5.2 The Environment

For now, the game will only feature a ground and some invisible walls at its edges. The ground itself will only be a large cube. Right-click in the Hierarchy tab and click 3D Object ➤ Cube. After the latter is selected, make sure its position and rotation are set to (0, 0, 0) in the Inspector tab. Give it a scale of (150, 0, 150). Figure 5-7 shows what its Transform should look like.

Figure 5-7. *The Transform component of the Ground GameObject*

Next, head over to Edit ➤ Project Settings ➤ Tags and Layers and create a Ground tag. Rename the Plane to Ground and assign it that tag. You can mark it as Static as well (Figure 5-8).

Figure 5-8. *Marking the Ground GameObject as Static*

For the invisible walls, create an empty GameObject, name it Walls, and reset its Transform component so that it has a position and rotation of (0, 0, 0) and a scale of (1, 1, 1). You can mark it as static too (Figure 5-9).

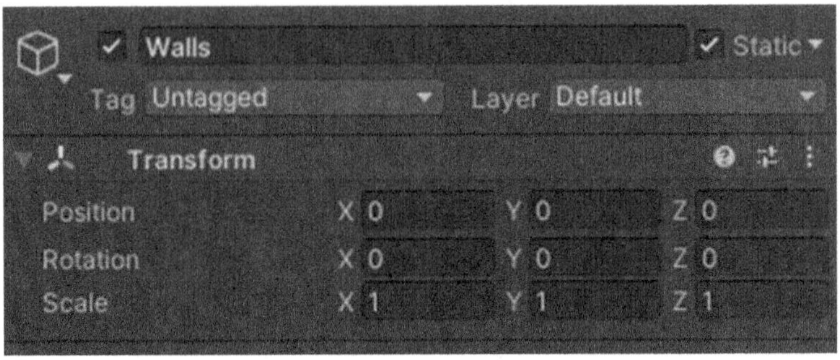

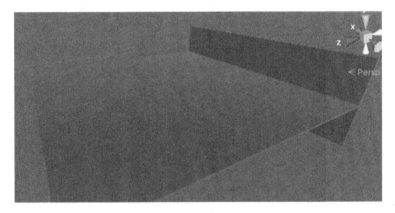

Figure 5-9. *The Transform component of the Walls GameObject*

Create a new cube GameObject as a child of Walls and name it Wall 1. Give it a position of (0, 0, -75), a rotation of (0, 0, 0), and a scale of (150, 50, 1). If you look at your Scene window, that cube should normally be at the forward edge of your ground (Figure 5-10).

Figure 5-10. *The Ground and Wall 1 GameObjects in the scene*

On the Wall 1 GameObject, disable its Mesh Renderer component (tick the check box beside its Mesh Renderer label), so that the wall can actually be invisible. Figure 5-11 shows all the components that are found on our first wall.

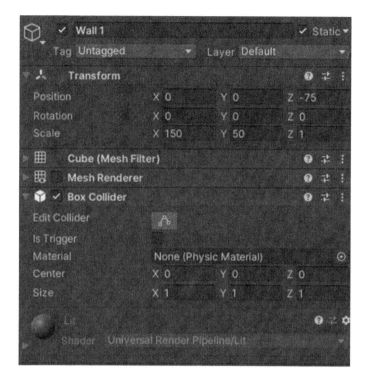

Figure 5-11. *The components on the Wall 1 GameObject*

Now, simply duplicate (Ctrl+D) the Wall 1 GameObject three times and place the new instances at the remaining edges of the ground. The following table will give you the necessary Transform values.

Name	Position	Rotation	Scale
Wall 1	(0, 0, -75)	(0, 0, 0)	(150, 50, 1)
Wall 2	(-75, 0, 0)	(0, 90, 0)	(150, 50, 1)
Wall 3	(0, 0, 75)	(0, 0, 0)	(150, 50, 1)
Wall 4	(75, 0, 0)	(0, 90, 0)	(150, 50, 1)

Here's what our hierarchy should look like so far (Figure 5-12):

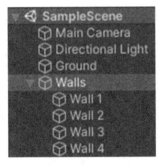

Figure 5-12. *GameObjects currently present in the scene, as seen in the hierarchy*

If you select the Walls GameObject or all of your actual 3D walls, your scene should look like this (Figure 5-13):

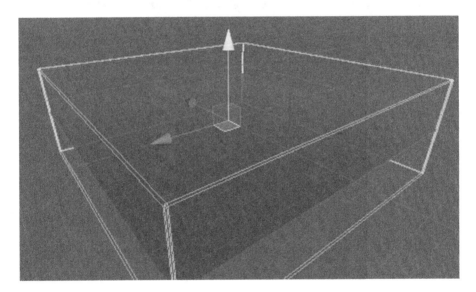

Figure 5-13. *Previewing the ground and invisible Walls GameObjects*

To complete this section, we just need to add some other kind of material to our ground. If it stays like this, the player might have difficulty perceiving that their tank is moving (if there's only the ground and the tank on the screen). As a solution, we could use a material with a Grid texture.

To make the game appear more interesting, let's use a stone texture with a cartoony look.

In your Project window, make two new folders: one named Materials and another named Textures. Then, head over to the Asset Store (Ctrl+9 or Window ➤ AssetStore), search for Stone Floor, sort by Price (Low to High), and download and import the asset shown in Figure 5-14.

If the asset is no longer available, download it from this link: `https://raw.githubusercontent.com/EdgeKing810/SphereShooter/master/Assets/Textures/Stone_floor_09.png`. Import it into the Editor by dragging and dropping it from your file manager to the Unity window in the Project window. Then, put the imported texture in a folder named Textures.

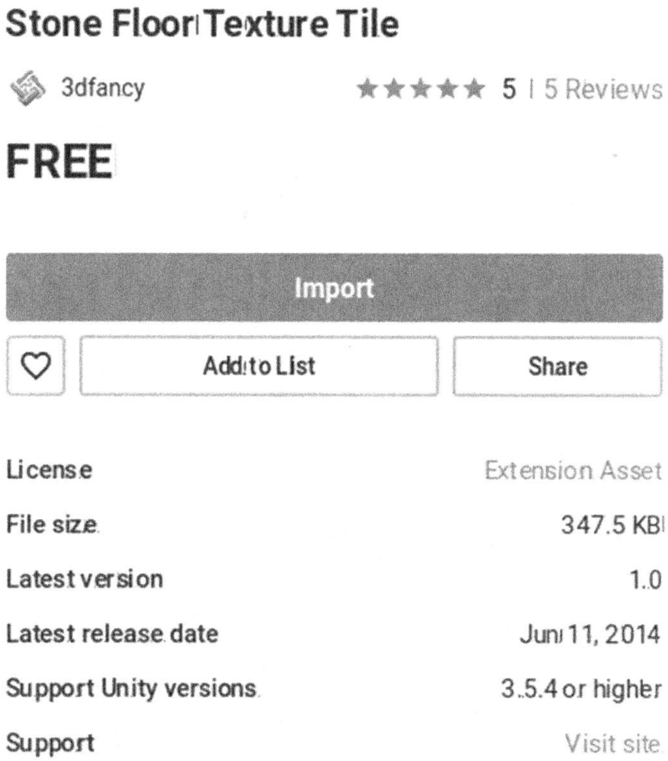

Stone Floor Texture Tile

3dfancy   ★ ★ ★ ★ ★ 5 | 5 Reviews

FREE

Import

♡	Add to List	Share

License	Extension Asset
File size	347.5 KB
Latest version	1.0
Latest release date	Jun 11, 2014
Support Unity versions	3.5.4 or higher
Support	Visit site

Figure 5-14. *The Stone Floor Texture Tile asset from the Asset Store*

A new folder named stone_floor_texture must have been formed when you imported the asset from the store. Move the Stone_floor_09 texture (square-looking one) to the Textures folder you created in the previous step (drag and drop) and delete the stone_floor_texture folder.

In your Materials folder, right-click and hit Create ➤ Material. Name it Ground. Drag and drop the Stone_floor_09 texture in the little square beside the Base Map label on the Ground material or click the circle icon beside that same label and select the texture. Set the color of the Base Map as RGBA (255, 255, 255, 255) or Hexadecimal FFFFFF. The Metallic and Smoothness sliders should each be set to 0, so that the game has a better look. Finally, set both of the Tilling values (X and Y) to 15 (Figure 5-15). This will make the texture repeat itself 15 times horizontally and vertically on our ground. Just drag and drop the material on the Ground GameObject in the Scene or Hierarchy window and save.

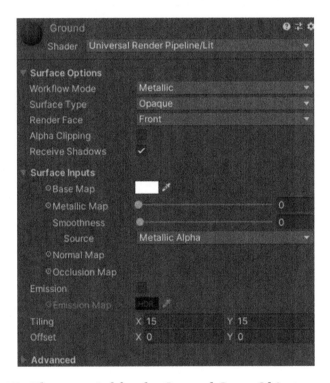

Figure 5-15. *The material for the Ground GameObject*

The ground should now look like that in Figure 5-16. Congratulations, our simple game environment is now ready!

Figure 5-16. *How your Ground GameObject should look*

5.3 Our Player (Tank)

In this section, we are going to create our player tank with a cube, a sphere, and a cylinder. We are also going to write our first scripts, to allow our tank to move, aim, and shoot with a twin-joystick setup.

5.3.1 Making the Tank

Refer to Figure 5-22 to get an idea of how our player tank will look.

1. Let's start by making a cube. Name it Player and give it a position of (0, 1, 0). Its rotation and scale will be the default (0, 0, 0) and (1, 1, 1), respectively.

2. Assign it the Player tag. (It already exists by default.)

3. Do not mark the Player tank as static, because that will stop it from moving later.

4. Make two new materials, name them as you wish, and give them a Base Map color of your choice. I will be making a Cyan (0, 110, 255) and a Yellow (255, 255, 255) material and will reduce their Metallic and Smoothness sliders to 0.

5. Drag and drop one of the two materials you created on the Player GameObject (in my case, the Cyan one).

6. Add a Rigidbody component to the Player and check all the constraints (except position X and Z), so that the Player tank doesn't rotate or move along/on axes we don't want (Figure 5-17).

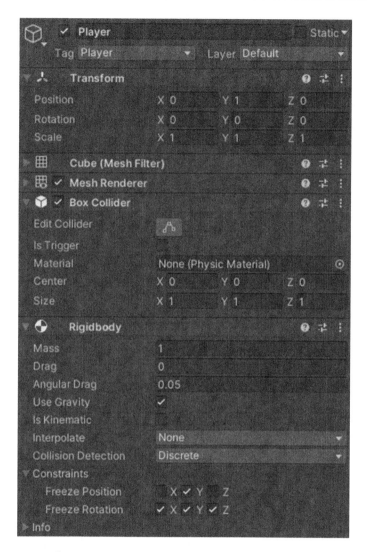

Figure 5-17.   *The components on the Player GameObject*

Now, create a sphere as a child of the Player GameObject. Label it
Rotator. In the next steps, it will receive a cylinder to mimic a tank turret,
and it will be the object that will rotate when the player (you) tries to aim.
Give it a position of (0, 0.5, 0), a rotation of (0, 0, 0), and a scale of (0.75,
0.75, 0.75). Remove its Sphere Collider component, and make it use the

153

second of the two materials we previously created. In my case, I will be giving it the Yellow material (Figure 5-18).

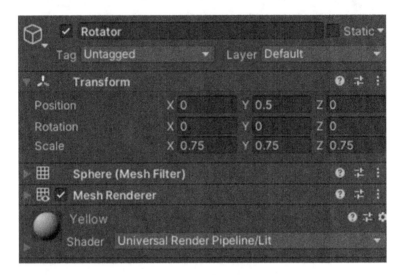

Figure 5-18. *The components on the Rotator GameObject*

To make the turret, create a Cylinder object as a child of the Rotator and name it Turret. Again, remove its Collider component (in this case, a Capsule Collider one) and give it the same material that is being used on the Rotator, to make it seem that these two objects make up a single one. The turret must have a position of (0, 0.2, 0.8), a rotation of (90, 0, 0), and a scale of (0.4, 0.8, 0.4) (Figure 5-19).

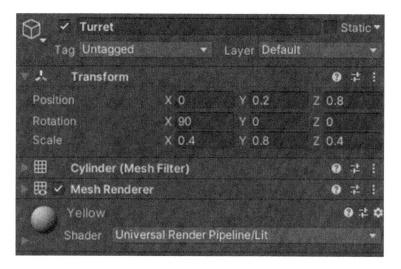

Figure 5-19. *The components on the Turret GameObject*

Our bullets need to exit from the tip of the turret. We will code this later, but for now, just create an empty GameObject as a child of the turret. It will have a position of (0, 1, 0), a rotation of (-90, 0, 0), and a scale of (1, 1, 1). Name it bulletEnd (Figure 5-20).

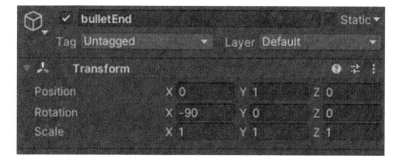

Figure 5-20. *The Transform component of the bulletEnd GameObject*

Your Hierarchy window should look like the following (Figure 5-21) at this point:

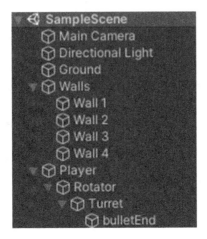

Figure 5-21. *The GameObjects currently present in our scene, as seen in the hierarchy*

The color that you chose for the player's tank might vary, but it should resemble Figure 5-22 at this stage.

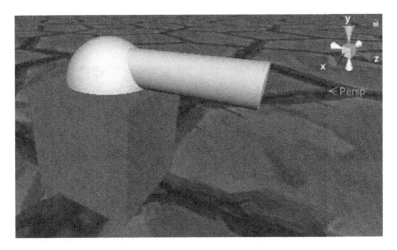

Figure 5-22. *How the player Tank GameObject looks*

5.3.2 Setting Up Our Scene

A quick and elegant solution to implement joystick-related behaviors in our game is to import the Simple Input System asset from the Asset Store (Figure 5-23).

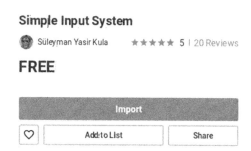

Simple Input System

Süleyman Yasir Kula   ★ ★ ★ ★ ★ 5 | 20 Reviews

FREE

Import

♡   Add to List   Share

Figure 5-23. *Importing the Simple Input System asset*

Next, we want to have two joysticks in our game: one for moving our tank and another for aiming its turret. Create a UI ➤ Canvas. Set its Canvas Scaler component to a Scale with Screen Size UI Scale mode. You're free to use a Reference Resolution and Screen Match Mode of your choice, but I will be using a 1920 × 1080 resolution and match only the height (1080) (Figure 5-24).

Figure 5-24.   *The components of the Canvas GameObject*

From your Project window, drag and drop the Plugins ➤ SimpleInput
➤ Prefabs ➤ Joystick prefab in your scene, as a child of the canvas. You'll
notice that the label of that new joystick has a bluish tint in your Hierarchy
window. This is because it is still currently a prefab. Any changes you
make to the Prefab (the instance in your Project window) will be applied
to any instance of it anywhere else—in your scenes, for example. We won't
require this capability, though. You can freely right-click the joystick in
your scene and click Unpack Prefab or Unpack Prefab completely. It will
just act like a regular GameObject then. Rename it Move Joystick.

Give the Move Joystick's Rect Transform a width and height of 300. Set
its position to (300, 300). Its child, named Thumb, should have a width and
height of 150 (Figure 5-25). Again, you're free to pick other values.

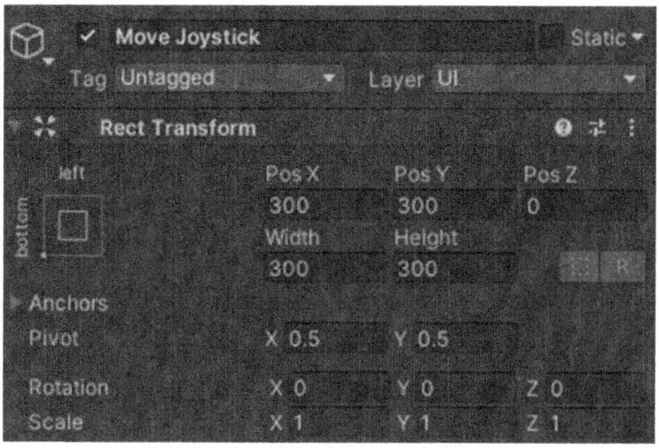

Figure 5-25. *The Rect Transform of Move Joystick*

There's no need to change any other properties, such as the pivot/anchor points of color of the Image component(s). You may also notice that there's a script attached to the joystick with the same name. This is the script that will be responsible for making the Joystick actually interactable and translating our actions to in-game inputs (Figure 5-26).

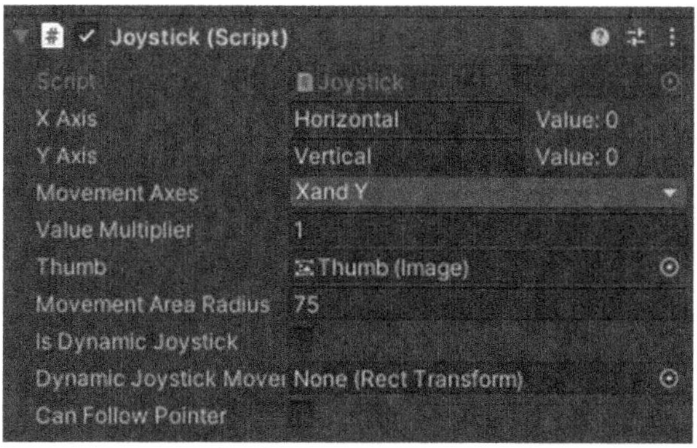

Figure 5-26. *The Joystick script of Move Joystick*

The X Axis and Y Axis fields translate to the name of the axis that will be used to represent -1 to 1 values of the joystick horizontally and vertically, respectively. The Value label will show its numeric value. The option

159

chosen in Movement Axes will define what axes the joystick will act on. Value Multiplier is pretty self-explanatory. If set to 5, the range of values for the joystick along one axis will be -5 to 5. Thumb represents the child of the joystick that will be the object that moves to provide visual feedback for the direction the player is pointing the joystick in. Movement Area Radius is the maximum distance from the center of the joystick that the Thumb can move to. Dynamic Joystick options just make the Joystick invisible after a certain delay, without interaction, and allow the player to make the joystick appear anywhere they touch the screen (or in a defined area).

We will let these options remain, as they are for the Move Joystick. Duplicate the Move Joystick GameObject, name the new instance Look Joystick, and position it at the same Y position, but at a different X position, that is equal to the same distance the Move Joystick was from the left edge of the screen, but this time, from the right edge. These Joystick GameObjects have a pivot point at the bottom-left corner that makes their X and Y positions relative to that point of the canvas. As I had set my screen width to be 1920 (in the Canvas Scaler), the new X position for my Look Joystick will be 1920 – 300, which is equal to 1620. Just change the axes of the script on the Look Joystick to be MouseX for the X Axis and MouseY for the Y Axis (Figure 5-27).

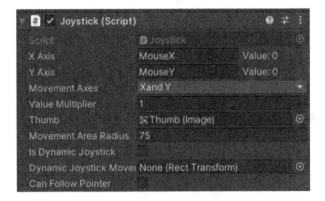

Figure 5-27. *The Joystick script of the Look Joystick*

Our game will be following a top-down camera view. To achieve that, place your Main Camera GameObject just above your tank and rotate it so that it looks down. My Main Camera has a position of (0, 12.5, 0), a rotation of (90, 0, 0), and a scale of (1, 1, 1). All of the other properties on its other components are set to their default values. I'm also going to set a Solid Color under Environment for its Camera component, so that when the tank reaches the edge of the ground, there is a more appropriate background. I'm using a Color of (60, 70, 60, 255) and, in hex, 3C463C (Figure 5-28).

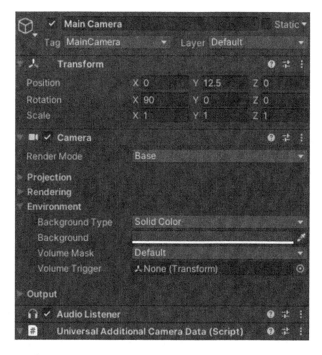

Figure 5-28. *The components on the Main Camera GameObject*

I also rotated my Directional Light, so that the shadows formed on the ground looked more appropriate to me (Figure 5-29). This is not required, however.

☑ **Directional Light**			Static ▾
Tag Untagged ▾		Layer Default	▾
⋏ **Transform**			❷ ⇅ ⋮
Position	X 0	Y 3	Z 0
Rotation	X 120	Y -30	Z 0
Scale	X 1	Y 1	Z 1

Figure 5-29. *The Transform component on my Directional Light GameObject*

Your Game window should look like the following screenshot (Figure 5-30), with the joysticks added and the camera repositioned/ rotated at this point.

Figure 5-30. *How the Game window should currently look*

5.3.3 Player Movement

Time to make our player tank actually move! To keep our Assets organized, create a new folder in your Project window named Scripts. In that folder, right-click and create a C# script. Name it playerMovement. Again, if you want to pick another application to edit scripts, head over to Edit ➤ Preferences ➤ External Tools and choose the one you want. Then, double-click on Script to open it.

In the last section of Chapter 3, I discussed the purpose of everything present in a blank Unity C# script, so I won't cover that again. First, add the line using SimpleInputNamespace; on the fourth line, just after using UnityEngine;. This will allow us to match the inputs on the axes of our joysticks to actual actions in the game.

As we did for the first line inside of our playerMovement class, we will create some variables to either hold values or reference other components. Also, we won't be using void Update() {}, and we will be removing all comments. Make your code look like the following:

```csharp
using System.Collections;
using System.Collections.Generic;
using UnityEngine;
using SimpleInputNamespace;

public class playerMovement : MonoBehaviour {
 public Transform rotator;
 private Rigidbody cubeRb;

 public float speed = 5.0f;

 private Vector2 input;

 void Start() {

 }
}
```

The `rotator` variable will reference a Transform component, which we'll later rotate, based on inputs, so that our tank can aim with its turret. As it is marked as public, we can assign it visually to our script ourselves, in the Inspector, later. `cubeRb` is a private variable and won't be visible in the Inspector. We will assign it the Rigidbody component of our player tank from the script itself. While there are many methods to move a character in a game, the one we will be using consists of modifying the velocity of our tank (its Rigidbody), based on the inputs from our Move Joystick.

The `speed` variable will contain a float value and be visible in the Inspector. We will be multiplying our joystick inputs to that value, to make the player tank move slower or faster.

Finally, we will be storing our inputs in a `Vector2` variable. As our tank will just be moving along the X and Z axes, we don't have to use a `Vector3` variable. Note that curly brackets can be placed on a new line (as they were by default) too. There's a lot that goes into personal preference when it comes to coding.

The script will be attached to our player tank and will act as a component later on. A lot of the movement or turret rotation it will perform will have to do with the Rigidbody of our player tank, which will be referenced in the `CubeRb` variable. To achieve this, we can add one line to our `Start` function, so that when the game starts, `cubeRb` is referenced.

```
void Start() {
  cubeRb = GetComponent<Rigidbody>();
}
```

That line can be interpreted as "Get the Rigidbody component on the current GameObject and reference it in our `cubeRb` variable." Now, every time we do something to the `cubeRb` variable, it will directly affect the Rigidbody component on our player tank. It is not necessary to use a variable, but it is more convenient than typing `GetComponent<Rigidbody>()` each time. We are also making savings in performance, by caching MonoBehaviour components in our current system.

To keep our code organized and clean, we will make use of many functions and have a more modular approach. To get joystick inputs, we will make use of the following function. You can add it just after the Start one.

```
bool GetInput(string horizontal, string vertical) {
 input.x = SimpleInput.GetAxisRaw(horizontal) * speed;
 input.y = SimpleInput.GetAxisRaw(vertical) * speed;

 return (Mathf.Abs(input.x) > 0.01f) || (Mathf.Abs(input.y) > 0.01f);
}
```

Basically, we are creating a function named GetInput. To it, we will be passing two strings, each corresponding to the horizontal and vertical axes of a joystick, respectively.

Then, we will be fetching the current numerical values of these axes using SimpleInput.GetAxisRaw(<axisName>), multiply them by the float value held in the speed variable, and store them in the X or Y position of input;, our Vector2 variable.

Additionally, the function will return a Boolean value. It will return true, if at least one of the two values of our Vector2 variable, input, is holding a value greater or less than but not equal to 0. A value of true being returned can be interpreted as "the joystick is being interacted with," because SimpleInput joysticks have a value of 0 on both their axes when not being held/touched.

As joystick axis inputs can be less than 0 (-1 to 1), we could formulate a formula such as "return true if horizontal axis is less than 0 or horizontal axis is greater than 0 or vertical axis is less than 0 or vertical axis is greater than 0, else return false," which, in UnityScript, would be written as follows:

```
if (input.x < 0 || input.x > 0 || input.y < 0 || input.y > 0) {
 return true;
} else {
 return false;
}
```

Perhaps you've noticed that the condition in the `if` statement itself will give a `true` or `false` value, so we can return that itself, instead of making a long or bulky `if-else` statement. Now the whole statement has been reduced to

```
return (input.x < 0 || input.x > 0 || input.y < 0 || input.y > 0);
```

We can further simplify that by making use of the `Mathf.Abs()` function, which is already available to us. The `Abs` part stands for "Absolute." This means that for any number that you pass to that function, it will return its absolute value. If you pass a positive value to it, there will be no changes, but if you pass a negative one, it will be converted into a positive number. For example, passing the 0, -9.88, 12.5, and -78.489 values one at a time to the function will return 0, 9.88, 12.5, and 78.489. That is how I obtained the return statement in the previous picture. Feel free to use any number of parentheses you want, to keep your code cleaner.

To actually move the player, we'll again create and use another function.

```
void MovePlayer() {
 cubeRb.velocity = Vector3.Normalize(new Vector3(input.x, 0,
 input.y)) * speed;
}
```

In short, we are going to set the velocity of the player tank's Rigidbody (by making use of the `cubeRb` variable that is referencing it) to match our horizontal and vertical inputs. As our Rigidbody requires a `Vector3` value for its velocity (in 3D axes), the Y value of our `Vector2` variable, `input`, will correspond to the Z axis here. We will also Normalize our `Vector3` value, so that the player tank doesn't go faster when moving diagonally. This will force our `Vector3` to have a magnitude of 1, so we will again have to multiply it by the value held in our speed variable. You'll also notice that we are not returning anything. This is because our function is marked `void`.

For context, we will be fetching the inputs once again but store them in the input `Vector2` variable itself later, for the axes responsible for rotating the turret. `rotator` is a variable referencing a GameObject with a Transform component (our sphere on top of our cube). We will want to rotate it about the Y axis. By default, rotation is expressed in a Quaternion format rather than a `Vector3` one. So, to rotate GameObjects in terms of `Vector3` using their Transform components, we need to modify their `eulerAngles` property.

```
void RotateTurret() {
 rotator.eulerAngles = new Vector3(0, Mathf.Atan2(input.x,
 input.y) * 180 / Mathf.PI, 0);
}
```

If you ever did a little trigonometry, you know that to find the angle between two lines, we use tan. We are doing exactly the same thing: finding the angle between the X and Y joystick inputs. As the angle we'll obtain is in a radian form, we must convert it to degrees. We can either multiply that value by 180 then divide it by pi (`Mathf.PI`) or just multiply it by `Mathf.Rad2Deg`, which essentially does the same thing. Finally, after obtaining that angle in degrees, we just create a new `Vector3` variable, give its Y value a value equal to our angle, and assign it to the `eulerAngles` property of the Transform of the GameObject we wish to rotate—in our case, our rotator.

To complete this script, we must call our functions, so that they're used. Previously, we discussed a game loop named `Update()`, which runs every frame and executes code placed within its curly brackets. As we're now dealing with rigidbodies and, thus, physics-related stuff, it's better to make use of another function named `FixedUpdate()`, which runs at intervals rather than every frame. This will make our game look smoother.

```
void FixedUpdate() {
 if (GetInput("Horizontal", "Vertical")) {
  MovePlayer();
}
```

```
if (GetInput("MouseX", "MouseY")) {
 RotateTurret();
 }
}
```

On the first lines, we're using the GetInput function, passing the "Horizontal" and "Vertical" axes. The input Vector2 variable will hold the current value of these two axes. The if statement will ensure that the MovePlayer() function will only be called if the player is currently interacting with the Move Joystick.

Similarly, we're calling the GetInput function again, but this time, passing the axes of the Look Joystick. If the player is interacting with the latter, only then the turret (rotator) will be rotated. If we didn't have this check, the turret would jump back to its original position (pointing up) each time we let go of the Look Joystick, which ruins the gameplay a bit.

Here's the full code, if you have been stuck somewhere. It is always recommended to type the code yourself, however. Functions do not have to be typed before or after another.

```
using System.Collections;
using System.Collections.Generic;
using UnityEngine;
using SimpleInputNamespace;

public class playerMovement : MonoBehaviour {
 public Transform rotator;
 private Rigidbody cubeRb;
 public float speed = 5.0f;
 private Vector2 input;

 void Start() {
  cubeRb = GetComponent<Rigidbody>();
 }
```

```
void FixedUpdate() {
 if (GetInput("Horizontal", "Vertical")) {
  MovePlayer();
 }

 if (GetInput("MouseX", "MouseY")) {
  RotateTurret();
 }
}

bool GetInput(string horizontal, string vertical) {
 input.x = SimpleInput.GetAxisRaw(horizontal) * speed;
 input.y = SimpleInput.GetAxisRaw(vertical) * speed;

 return (Mathf.Abs(input.x) > 0.01f) || (Mathf.Abs(input.y) >
 0.01f);
}

void MovePlayer() {
 cubeRb.velocity = Vector3.Normalize(new Vector3(input.x, 0,
 input.y)) * speed;
}

void RotateTurret() {
 rotator.eulerAngles = new Vector3(0, Mathf.Atan2(input.x,
 input.y) * 180 / Mathf.PI, 0);
 }
}
```

Just save the script and head back to the Unity Editor when you're done. Drag and drop the script on the player tank or Add Component ➤ playerMovement. While the player tank is selected, drag and drop the Rotator GameObject from the hierarchy in the rotator field of the script. Enter the Play mode and try interacting with the Move and Look joysticks. One should cause the player tank to move and go in the specified direction, while the other should cause the turret to appear to be rotating.

5.3.4 Camera Positioning

While testing the game in the last section, you might have noticed that the player tank can go offscreen. This is not something we want, so, in this section, we will configure Main Camera to follow the player tank smoothly. This time, create a script named cameraFollow and open it.

We will use only two variables: a Transform one named player, which will be referencing the Transform of our player tank, and a float one, height.

```
public Transform player;
public float height = 12.5f;
```

To make the camera follow the player, we must use a function such as Update() and set the position of the camera to that of the player, except for the Y value, which, instead, we'll set to the value held in our height variable, so that we can have a proper top-down view.

```
void LateUpdate() {
  this.transform.position = new Vector3(player.position.x,
height, player.position.z);
}
```

Instead of the traditional Update(), we will be using LateUpdate(), which is very similar but runs after other update loops have been run. Placing camera-movement related code in it is a good practice, because it means that all the movement-related code has already been executed first, before the camera has to move. Again, here's the full code:

```
using System.Collections;
using System.Collections.Generic;
using UnityEngine;
```

```
public class cameraFollow : MonoBehaviour {

 public Transform player;
 public float height = 12.5f;

 void LateUpdate() {
  this.transform.position = new Vector3(player.position.x,
  height, player.position.z);
 }
}
```

Save the script, add it to the Main Camera GameObject, and drag and drop the Player GameObject from the hierarchy to the player field of the script and hit the Play button. The camera should follow the player tank now.

5.3.5 Making the Player Shoot Bullets

This section is divided into two parts: making the bullet and shooting. To make the bullet, simply create a sphere (3D Object ➤ Sphere) GameObject in your hierarchy first. Name it Bullet and give it a position of (0, 1, 2), a rotation of (0, 0, 0), and a scale of (0.3, 0.3, 0.3). Next, make a tag named Bullet and assign it to your GameObject. Also, under Lighting properties in the Mesh Renderer component of the Bullet GameObject, set Cast Shadows to Off, so that bullets do not appear to have a shadow (Figure 5-31).

Figure 5-31. *The components on the Bullet GameObject #1*

Leave the Sphere Collider properties as they are, then add a Rigidbody component to the Bullet GameObject. Untick Use Gravity and tick only the Freeze Position Y under constraints. You might also want to create/add a material to the Bullet GameObject at this point. I will be using the Light Green one (Figure 5-32).

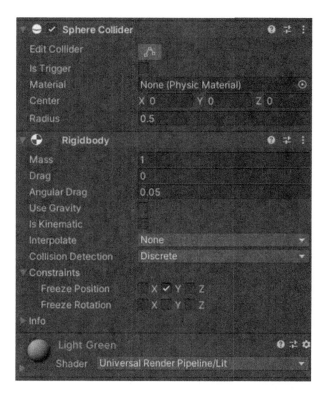

Figure 5-32. *The components on the Bullet GameObject #2*

Finally, we will want our bullets to get destroyed eventually, so that they don't always remain in our game and cause a drop in performance. To do this, create a script named destroyer, wait for it to finish compiling (see the small loading icon in the bottom-right corner), and then add it on the Bullet component. Open the script. Here's the full code:

```
using System.Collections;
using System.Collections.Generic;
using UnityEngine;
```

```
public class destroyer : MonoBehaviour {
 public float delay = 3.0f;

 void Start() {
  Destroy(this.gameObject, delay);
 }
}
```

On the first line, inside of the class, we're creating a new public float variable named delay and giving it an initial value of 3. Then, in the Start function of our script, we're telling Unity to Destroy the GameObject that script is attached to, after a number of seconds that correspond to the value currently being held in the delay variable. If we don't pass any second parameters to the Destroy function, it will immediately destroy our GameObject as soon as the game starts. Finally, in your project window, create a folder named Prefabs and drag and drop the Bullet GameObject from your hierarchy to that folder. You have successfully made a prefab! You can now safely destroy the Bullet GameObject from your scene.

For the next steps, you will also require a sound effect to be played when you shoot bullets. You can use the one I will be using, by downloading it from https://raw.githubusercontent.com/EdgeKing810/SphereShooter/master/Assets/Sounds/fireBullets.wav (right-click and Save As). Make a folder named Sounds or Sound Effects and drag and drop the .wav file or the sound file you will be using from your file manager to the Unity Editor. Next, add an Audio Source component to your player tank GameObject, untick Play On Awake, and assign the audio file you just imported in the AudioClip property (Figure 5-33).

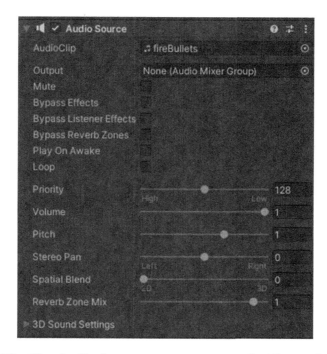

Figure 5-33. *The Audio Source component on the Player GameObject*

Time to give our player tank the ability to shoot bullets! Create a new script named bulletSystem and open it. Interacting with the Look joystick right now is only causing the rotator to rotate, thus aiming the turret in the direction we want. However, if we want to shoot, the handle (Thumb) of that joystick will have to be more than a defined distance from the center of the joystick. Next, we will want to check if enough time has passed since the player has last shot, to be able to shoot again. Finally, if those two conditions are satisfied, we just have to instantiate (spawn) a bullet at the bulletEnd position (the empty GameObject that is a child of our turret), give that bullet a force, to propel it forward, and emit a shooting sound.

First, add the Using SimpleInputNamespace; line to the script, because we will be fetching joystick inputs later too. Here are the variables that we will be using in this script:

```
public Transform bulletEnd;
public Rigidbody bulletPrefab;

public float force = 500.0f;

float currentTime;
public float delay = 0.5f;

AudioSource audioSource;
```

bulletEnd will be referencing the Transform component of the child of our Turret GameObject for where bullets should be instantiated. Unsurprisingly, bulletPrefab will reference the Bullet prefab that we created. The floating value in the force variable will define the force at which bullets that have been instantiated will be propulsed. currentTime and delay represent, respectively, the number of seconds since the start of the game that the last bullet was fired and the number of seconds the player must wait to fire another bullet. Last, the audioSource private variable will reference the Audio Source on the player tank to play the assigned sound effect later.

```
void Start() {
 audioSource = GetComponent<AudioSource>();
}
```

In the Start function, we will just be referencing the Audio Source on the GameObject the script is attached to (our player tank) in the audioSource variable.

As our script has to deal with applying forces and, thus, physics, we'll use FixedUpdate.

```
void FixedUpdate() {
 if (((Mathf.Abs(SimpleInput.GetAxisRaw("MouseX")) > 0.75f) ||
      (Mathf.Abs(SimpleInput.GetAxisRaw("MouseY")) > 0.75f)) &&
    ((Time.time - currentTime > delay) || (currentTime < 0.01f))) {

    currentTime = Time.time;
    audioSource.Play();

    Rigidbody bulletInstance = Instantiate(bulletPrefab,
    bulletEnd.position, bulletEnd.rotation) as Rigidbody;
    bulletInstance.AddForce(bulletEnd.forward * force);
  }
 }
}
```

Let's first analyze the condition that allows all the instructions in the FixedUpdate loop to be run if true only.

```
((Mathf.Abs(SimpleInput.GetAxisRaw("MouseX")) > 0.75f) ||
(Mathf.Abs(SimpleInput.GetAxisRaw("MouseY")) > 0.75f))
```

This statement results in true only if MouseX and/or MouseY currently have a value greater than 0.75 or less than 0.75. In preceding sections, I have explained similar statements for the playerMovement script. Next, we're chaining the boolean we got from that statement with the following one:

```
((Time.time - currentTime > delay) || (currentTime < 0.01f))
```

This condition will return true only if more seconds than the value held in the delay variable have passed since the last time a bullet was fired, or if currentTime is less than 0.01, which means that it is the first time we're firing a bullet (so no need to wait). If both of these conditions are true (hence the && symbol), only then will we run the code within the if statement.

The first two lines that will be run will assign the value of the amount of seconds that have passed since the game was started to the currentTime variable, to indicate that the last time a bullet was fired was now, and play the AudioClip assigned in the AudioSource component.

Finally, we are creating a new Rigidbody variable named bulletInstance, and as we instantiate (make a clone of) the bullet prefab at the bulletEnd position and rotation in our scene, we assign it to that variable. bulletInstance, which is now holding a copy of our bullet prefab in the scene, will be given a force equal to the value present in the similarly named variable and in the forward direction of our turret (or bulletEnd, for that case).

Following is the full code, in case you missed something. Save the script and return to the Unity Editor.

```
using System.Collections;
using System.Collections.Generic;
using UnityEngine;
using SimpleInputNamespace;

public class bulletSystem : MonoBehaviour {
 public Transform bulletEnd;
 public Rigidbody bulletPrefab;

 public float force = 500.0f;

 float currentTime;
 public float delay = 0.5f;

 AudioSource audioSource;

 void Start() {
 audioSource = GetComponent<AudioSource>();
 }
```

```
void FixedUpdate() {
if (((Mathf.Abs(SimpleInput.GetAxisRaw("MouseX")) > 0.75f) ||
(Mathf.Abs(SimpleInput.GetAxisRaw("MouseY")) > 0.75f)) &&
((Time.time - currentTime > delay) || (currentTime < 0.01f))) {

  currentTime = Time.time;
  audioSource.Play();

  Rigidbody bulletInstance = Instantiate(bulletPrefab,
  bulletEnd.position, bulletEnd.rotation) as Rigidbody;
  bulletInstance.AddForce(bulletEnd.forward * force);
 }
}
}
```

Assign the script to the player tank GameObject. Expand the children of the Player GameObject in the hierarchy and drag and drop the bulletEnd GameObject in the Bullet End field of the script instance on the Player GameObject. In a similar fashion, drag and drop the Bullet GameObject from the Project window in the Bullet Prefab field. Enter Play mode and test that everything works. You should be able to shoot bullets now.

5.4 Enemies

In this section, we are going to make a spherical enemy, instantiate copies of it in our game, and make these copies target and move toward our player tank. Enemies should also be destroyed when they collide with either the player or with bullet(s). Let's take the first step right away.

5.4.1 Making an Enemy

Start by creating a sphere. Create and assign it a tag of Enemy and name the new sphere GameObject itself Enemy. Place it at a position of (0, 1.15, 10), and give it a rotation of (0, 0, 0) and a scale of (1.5, 1.5, 1.5). No properties are required to be modified for its Mesh Renderer or Sphere Collider components. Next, add a Rigidbody component, untick Use Gravity, and freeze the Y position of the GameObject from the Constraints tab.

Additionally, add an Audio Source component and untick Play On Awake. This Audio Source component will be from where sounds of the enemy getting destroyed will be played. Download the following audio file and import it in the previously created Sounds folder of the project:

https://github.com/EdgeKing810/SphereShooter/blob/master/
Assets/Sounds/explosion0.wav.

Assign explosion0 in the Audio Clip field of the Audio Source. You might also want to create/place a material on the Enemy GameObject at this point. I will be creating and using a red one (Figures 5-34 and 5-35).

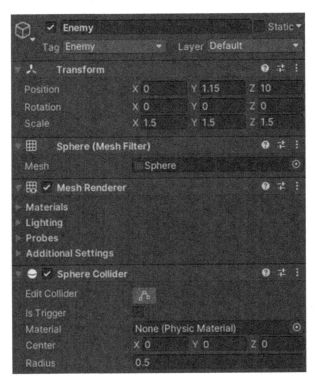

Figure 5-34. *The components on the Enemy GameObject #1*

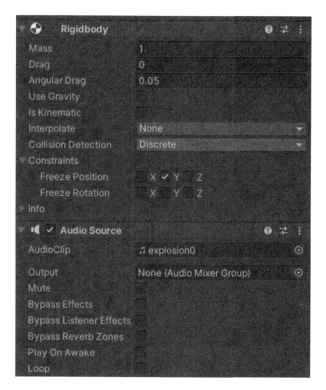

Figure 5-35. *The components on the Enemy GameObject #2*

To make our gameplay look a bit more interesting, let's add a Trail Renderer to our Enemy. For a reason that I'll explain later at the scripting stage, make a new empty GameObject as a child of our Enemy GameObject and name it Trail Renderer. Only edit its Transform component, and place it at a position of (0, 0, 0). If we placed it too high, the trail renderer would be rendered on top of our player tank.

Add a Trail Renderer component to that child GameObject. Try setting a width value of about 0.35 (right-click first, to set exact values) on the graph-looking thing, assign it a material of your choice at the Element 0 position under Materials, and set Cast Shadows to Off, under Lighting (Figures 5-36 and 5-37).

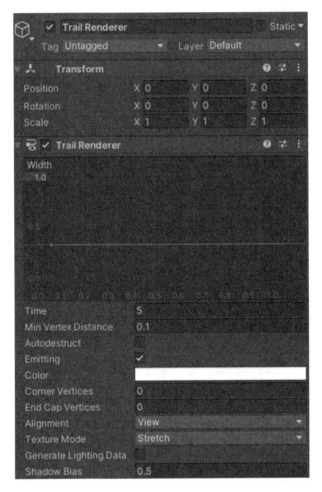

Figure 5-36. *The components on the Trail Renderer GameObject #1*

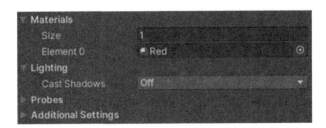

Figure 5-37. *The components on the Trail Renderer GameObject #2*

5.4.2 Importing Another Asset from the Store

When our Enemy collides with our player or a bullet, we will want to destroy it (which we can already do using `Destroy()`). We can also add some visual effects, such as an explosion particle system. Fortunately, there is a package on the Asset Store that provides everything we'll need. Download and import the Simple FX asset (Figure 5-38).

Figure 5-38.   *The Simple FX—Cartoon Particles asset in the Asset Store*

5.4.3 Making Our Enemy Move and Explode

Everything that enemies need to be able to handle and do will be put into only one script. Create and open a script named enemy from your Scripts folder. We will be making and using many variables.

```
const string playerTag = "Player";
const string bulletTag = "Bullet";
public float minSpeed = 1.0f;
public float maxSpeed = 6.0f;
```

```
float speed;
GameObject player;
public GameObject enemyExplosionPrefab;
AudioSource audioSource;
```

The tags that our player and bullets are using will be stored in two string constants identified respectively as playerTag and bulletTag. As we will be using these constants further on in our code, it will be easier to reference them in the long term using these constants, because if we change the tags of these GameObjects in the future, we will only have the value being held in these constants, rather than all references in our code.

Another thing that we will be doing is allow our enemies to move at a random speed, to make the game more fun. This random speed will be within the range of two float values contained in the minSpeed and maxSpeed variables and stored in a variable named speed, for later use.

The player GameObject variable will be used to contain a reference to our player tank GameObject. As enemies will be made using prefabs and instantiated in our scene in further sections, it will be useless to make the player variable public, because we won't be able to drag and drop the player from our scene to our enemy prefab in our project. Doing so doesn't make sense, as, for example, if a different scene is opened, a prefab can't reference a GameObject from that scene. Instead, we will be coding something with which the enemy can automatically find the player when it is instantiated.

The next GameObject variable is enemyExplosionPrefab and will be used to reference an explosion prefab from the Simple FX asset we imported earlier.

audioSource is simply a variable that will reference the Audio Source component on the Enemy to play the explosion sound we assigned to it in its Audio Clip field.

We are going to place some code in our Start function, so that it is executed only once, at the start of the lifespan of our enemy GameObjects.

```
void Start() {
 speed = Random.Range(minSpeed, maxSpeed);
 audioSource = GetComponent<AudioSource>();
 player = GameObject.FindWithTag(playerTag);
}
```

First, we are going to calculate a random speed from the minimum and maximum values we have set and store that float value in the speed variable, using the Random.Range function. Random.Range will return a random value greater or equal to minSpeed but less than maxSpeed.

Next, we are going to store a reference to the Audio Source component on the current GameObject (in our case, the one of our Enemy) in the audioSource variable. We are also making use of the GameObject.FindWithTag function, passing the string in the playerTag constant as parameter, to reference the GameObject of our player tank in the player. GameObject.FindWithTag will search for a GameObject having the tag we passed as parameter, and as soon as it finds one meeting that criteria, it will return it.

For the game loop, we can either make use of Update or FixedUpdate.

```
void FixedUpdate() {
 if (player) {
  transform.position = Vector3.MoveTowards(transform.position,
  player.transform.position, speed * Time.deltaTime);
 } else {
  GetComponent<Rigidbody>().velocity = new Vector3(0, 0, 0);
 }
}
```

In `FixedUpdate`, we will perform one of two actions, depending on whether there is a player tank GameObject in our scene. If, for example, our player tank GameObject is destroyed in the current scene, the `player` variable will hold a value of `null` instead of an actual GameObject reference.

A way to check "if the `player` variable is currently referencing a GameObject" could be `if (player != null)` or simply `if (player)`. Logically, if the `player` variable does not have a `null` value, it must correspond to a GameObject, in our case, the player tank, because it is the only GameObject that uses the value held in the `playerTag` constant as tag.

So, if the `player` variable actually corresponds to something, we want the Enemy to move toward the position held in its Transform component. To do this, we can simply set the value of the position of the Transform of our Enemy GameObject to be equal to the `Vector3` value returned by the `Vector3.MoveTowards` function. In our case, `Vector3.MoveTowards` uses three parameters. The first is the a `Vector3` value (the current position of our Enemy), which we want to gradually turn into the value passed as the second parameter (the position of the player tank). The third value defines the rate or speed at which we want the first value to turn into the second; hence, we pass the `speed` variable. A `Vector3` value closer to that of the position of the player will be returned every time `FixedUpdate` runs. Multiplying the value by `Time.deltaTime` makes the transition more linear and smoother when using `Update` as it runs each frame. It won't make a difference in `FixedUpdate`.

Otherwise, if our `player` variable corresponds to `null`, we will want to make our Enemy GameObject stop moving and stay in place. If we hadn't included that `if` statement in the first place, we would have received many errors if the player tank GameObject was destroyed, because the script would try to move the Enemy to a position of `null`, which is invalid.

We will also make use of two other functions. The next is `OnCollisionEnter`, which will run automatically in our script when the enemy collides with anything. The parameter we pass to this function corresponds to the collision caused by the Collider of the GameObject that collided with that of the GameObject that the script was on caused. In our case, that parameter will be equal to the collision caused by the Collider of any GameObject that collides with (the collider of) our Enemy GameObject. We will just reference the collision that Collider caused as the local variable col.

```
void OnCollisionEnter(Collision col) {
 if (col.gameObject.CompareTag(bulletTag)) {
  Destroy(col.gameObject);
 }

 if (col.gameObject.CompareTag(playerTag) ||
     col.gameObject.CompareTag(bulletTag)) {
  DestroyEnemy();
 }
}
```

The first if condition checks whether the GameObject that collided with our Enemy was a Bullet GameObject. We do this by accessing the GameObject of the Collider that caused the collision and then checking whether it has the same tag as Bullet GameObjects, using the string value held in the bulletTag constant as parameter. We could also write if (col.gameObject.tag == bulletTag), but the way I wrote it is the recommended way, which also provides some performance benefits.

If that is the case, we will wish to destroy the Bullet GameObject that just collided. In the next if condition, we check whether the Enemy GameObject collided with a bullet or with the player tank. If that is what happened, we want to call a function named DestroyEnemy that will determine what should happen when the enemy "dies."

```
void DestroyEnemy() {
 GameObject explosionInstance = Instantiate(enemyExplosionP
 refab, transform.position, enemyExplosionPrefab.transform.
 rotation);
 Destroy(explosionInstance, 5.0f);

 audioSource.Play();

 Transform trailRenderer = transform.GetChild(0);
 if (trailRenderer) {
  trailRenderer.parent = null;
  Destroy(trailRenderer.gameObject,    trailRenderer.
  GetComponent<TrailRenderer>().time);
 }

Destroy(this.gameObject);
}
```

In the DestroyEnemy function, the first thing that we will do is instantiate the enemy explosion prefab GameObject from Simple FX, referenced in the enemyExplosionPrefab variable, at the position of the Enemy GameObject, but at the rotation of the explosion prefab itself, and store a reference to that instance in a new local GameObject variable that we will create and name explosionInstance.

After the explosion particle system has been instantiated and run in the scene, instead of bloating our scene with many GameObjects that serve no purpose, we'll instead destroy the GameObject of that explosion particle system after five seconds (just ample time for the system to fully run). Then, we will play the Audio Clip held in the enemy's Audio Source component (explosion0).

As we want our Trail Renderer to be wiped out automatically, instead of being immediately destroyed when our Enemy is "dead," we create a reference to it in a new Transform variable called trailRenderer. Calling transform.GetChild(0) returns the first child (0 being the first index) of the current GameObject's (our Enemy GameObject) transform.

Next, if the enemy has a child GameObject, trailRenderer shouldn't be equal to null. Only then will we set the parent of the trailRenderer GameObject or the first child of our Enemy GameObject to be equal to null. This will make the GameObject have no parent at all and, thus, not be the child of any GameObject anymore. However, as I discussed earlier, with the instance of the explosion GameObject, we will destroy the trailRenderer's GameObject too, but this time, instead of thinking of and putting a suitable value, we will fetch the amount of time that the Trail Renderer component itself will take to wipe its trail out or, in other words, the amount of time it will take for the trail to reach a length/width of 0 and pass it as second parameter to the Destroy function, which will cause the Trail Renderer's GameObject to be destroyed as soon as it has a trail length/width of 0. Remember that trails will autodestroy parts of themselves with time by default. Now, you might understand why we made a new GameObject for the Trail Renderer component earlier, instead of placing it on the main Enemy GameObject.

Last, we immediately destroy the GameObject of the enemy. Here is the full script:

```
using System.Collections;
using System.Collections.Generic;
using UnityEngine;

public class enemy : MonoBehaviour {
 const string playerTag = "Player";
 const string bulletTag = "Bullet";
 public float minSpeed = 1.0f;
 public float maxSpeed = 6.0f;
 float speed;
 GameObject player;
```

```
public GameObject enemyExplosionPrefab;
AudioSource audioSource;

void Start() {
 speed = Random.Range(minSpeed, maxSpeed);
 audioSource = GetComponent<AudioSource>();
 player = GameObject.FindWithTag(playerTag);
}

void FixedUpdate() {
 if (player) {
  transform.position = Vector3.MoveTowards(transform.position,
  player.transform.position, speed * Time.deltaTime);
 } else {
  GetComponent<Rigidbody>().velocity = new Vector3(0, 0, 0);
 }
}

void OnCollisionEnter(Collision col) {
 if (col.gameObject.CompareTag(bulletTag)) {
  Destroy(col.gameObject);
 }

 if (col.gameObject.CompareTag(playerTag) ||
     col.gameObject.CompareTag(bulletTag)) {
  DestroyEnemy();
 }
}

void DestroyEnemy() {
 GameObject explosionInstance = Instantiate(enemyExplosion
 Prefab, transform.position, enemyExplosionPrefab.transform.
 rotation);
 Destroy(explosionInstance, 5.0f);
```

```
 audioSource.Play();

 Transform trailRenderer = transform.GetChild(0);
 if (trailRenderer) {
  trailRenderer.parent = null;
  Destroy(trailRenderer.gameObject,    trailRenderer.
  GetComponent<TrailRenderer>().time);
 }

 Destroy(this.gameObject);
 }
}
```

Save the script. When you're back in the Unity Editor, put the
script on the Enemy GameObject and drag and drop the SimpleFX ➤
Prefabs ➤ FX_Fireworks_Blue_Small prefab, or a similar one, in the
enemyExplosionPrefab field on the script. If you hit Play, you should see
that the sole enemy in our scene will move toward the player tank and play
a sound and spawn an explosion when it is destroyed, either by being hit
by a bullet or by colliding with the Player GameObject. In Chapter 6, we
are going to improve the game by randomly spawning some enemies at
set spawn points, adding health (for the player) and high scores, making a
menu for when the game starts and when a player loses, and much more.

Improving and Building Sphere Shooter

While technically the game is playable as configured in the previous chapter, in this chapter, we will add several new mechanics and features. At the end, I will discuss additional features that can be included in the game, if you wish to continue to develop it and trigger a build, so that we have a standalone app that can be installed on Android devices.

6.1 Spawning Enemies

One enemy is nice, but the game would be way better if we had more. In this section, we will place empty GameObjects at defined positions in our scene and, at a set delay, instantiate (spawn) enemies at a random position of the defined ones.

Create an empty GameObject, name it SpawnPoints, and place it at a position of (0, 1.15, 0). Its rotation and scale will already be set at (0, 0, 0) and (1, 1, 1). We could mark it as static, but that wouldn't make a difference.

Create four empty GameObjects as children of SpawnPoints (Figure 6-1). Name them how you want, and place them at (0, 0, 15), (15, 0, 0), (0, 0, -15), and (-15, 0, 0).

© Kishan Takoordyal 2020
K. Takoordyal, *Beginning Unity Android Game Development*,
https://doi.org/10.1007/978-1-4842-6002-9_6

Figure 6-1. *SpawnPoint GameObjects*

Next, drag and drop the Enemy GameObject from the scene to the Prefabs folder in the Project window and delete it from the scene.

Create a new script, name it enemySpawner, wait for it to compile, place it on the SpawnPoints GameObject in the scene, and open it. This is what will be responsible for spawning enemies in our scene.

```
public float delay;
public GameObject enemy;
```

We will store the delay between spawning enemies in a public float variable named delay and store a reference to our enemy Prefab GameObject in enemy.

```
void SpawnEnemy() {
    int randomPos = (int)Random.Range(0, transform.childCount);
    Instantiate(enemy, transform.GetChild(randomPos).position,
    enemy.transform.rotation);
}
```

To spawn enemies, we will make use of a function named SpawnEnemy. The first thing that we will do in that function is pick the index of one of the children of the SpawnPoints GameObject randomly. There are four possible spawn points available, so we pass the minimum (0) and the maximum (transform.childCount) to the Random.Rage function, to randomly select one. By doing this, we can add as many spawn points as we wish without editing the code every time. As the value that is going to be returned will be a floating-point one, we convert it to an integer (casting) and store it in the local variable randomPos. In the next step, we find the child of SpawnPoints at the index we just got and instantiate an Enemy GameObject at that position and at the enemy's rotation itself.

```
void Start() {
    InvokeRepeating("SpawnEnemy", 0.0f, delay);
}
```

Finally, the SpawnEnemy function will be called as soon as the game starts at every <delay> seconds, using the InvokeRepeating function, which takes the following three parameters:

1. The function to call

2. The start time

3. How often the function should be called

```
using System.Collections;
using System.Collections.Generic;
using UnityEngine;

public class enemySpawner : MonoBehaviour {
    public float delay;
    public GameObject enemy;

    void Start() {
        InvokeRepeating("SpawnEnemy", 0.0f, delay);
    }

    void SpawnEnemy() {
        int randomPos = (int)Random.Range(0, transform.childCount);
        Instantiate(enemy, transform.GetChild(randomPos).
        position, enemy.transform.rotation);
    }
}
```

Just set a delay value of your choice and drag and drop the Enemy prefab in the enemy field back in the Editor. Test to see if enemies are being spawned, moving toward the player tank, and being destroyed (Figure 6-2).

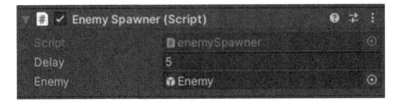

Figure 6-2. *The enemySpawner script as a component*

6.2 Scoring

Right now, when we kill an enemy, it just gets destroyed and disappears. However, it would be great if we could keep something like a score and increment it as enemies are killed.

To start, create a UI Text element under the Canvas GameObject. Name it ScoreText, place it at (-660, 350, 0), and give it a width and height of 375 and 100, respectively (Figure 6-3).

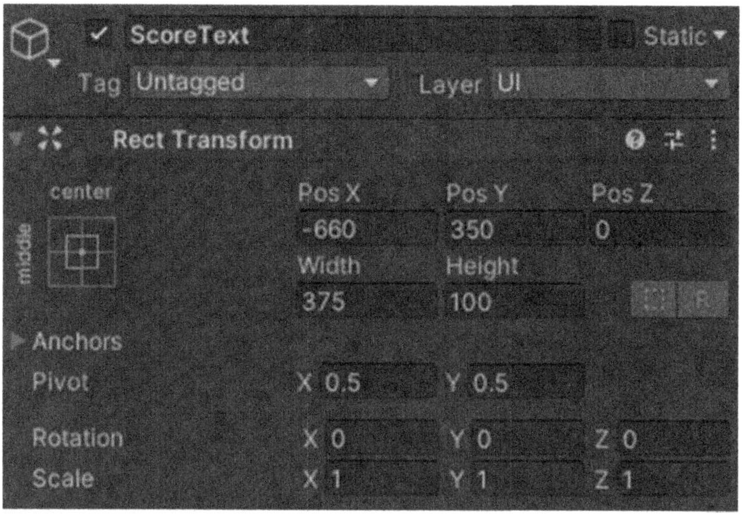

Figure 6-3. *The Rect Transform component of the ScoreText UI element*

For the Text component itself, we won't be using Best Fit, because it can look a bit awkward that the Text UI element in the game seems to get bigger/smaller as we play. So, instead, we set the font size to a maximum value that is anticipated to be sufficient to hold all the information we'll ever want to store in that UI element.

I have also added dummy text, as well as setting Font Style to Bold. Additionally, I have set text alignment to the left horizontally and in the center vertically and given it a yellowish color (Figure 6-4).

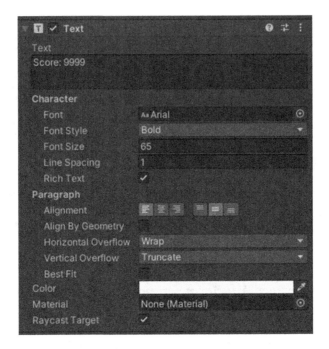

Figure 6-4. *The Text component of the ScoreText UI element*

We will want our enemies to send a call, to increase the score every time they get hit by a bullet and, correspondingly, update the ScoreText UI element. As I previously noted, we can't directly reference things in a scene to Prefabs in the Project window. This is a very good time to introduce Instances. Using static properties and making them publicly accessible in a scene, classes and functions can be accessed and called from anywhere in that scene.

To demonstrate this, create a new GameObject, name it ScriptManager, and create and open a script named scoreManager. Add the `using UnityEngine.UI` line to the script, so that we are able to modify the `text` value of `scoreText` later.

```
public static scoreManager instance;
public Text scoreText;
int score;
```

We will be using three variables. The first will be named `instance` and will literally correspond to an instance of our script that can be called from other scripts. The two other variables, `scoreText` and `score`, respectively, reference the UI Text element we previously created and configured and store the current score.

```
void UpdateScore() {
    scoreText.text = "Score: " + score.ToString();
}
```

We will have a function to update the contents of `scoreText` too, so that we don't have to continuously check or update using a form of the `Update()` function. Note that the contents in the score variable has to be converted into a string format.

```
void Awake() {
    if (instance) {
        Destroy(this.gameObject);
    } else {
        instance = this;
    }
    UpdateScore();
}

public void IncreaseScore(int amount) {
    score += amount;
    UpdateScore();
}
```

In the Awake function, we will create the instance for the script before other scripts have been initialized in the scene. We first check whether an instance of this script already exists, and if yes, we destroy the current one. Otherwise, we set the instance of the script in the scene to be the current one. Finally, we update our `scoreText`, so that it doesn't hold our dummy text at Play.

```
public void IncreaseScore(int amount) {
    score += amount;
    UpdateScore();
}
```

We will also have a last function, so that we can change the score value. To that function, we can pass a value to specify the amount by which to increment the score. We only have to update scoreText then.

```
using System.Collections;
using System.Collections.Generic;
using UnityEngine;
using UnityEngine.UI;

public class scoreManager : MonoBehaviour {
    public static scoreManager instance;
    public Text scoreText;
    int score;

    void Awake() {
        if (instance) {
            Destroy(this.gameObject);
        } else {
            instance = this;
        }
        UpdateScore();
    }

    public void IncreaseScore(int amount) {
        score += amount;
        UpdateScore();
    }
```

```
void UpdateScore() {
    scoreText.text = "Score: " + score.ToString();
}
}
```

Back in the Editor, we place the script on the ScriptManager GameObject and drag the actual ScoreText UI element in the `scoreText` field of the script (Figure 6-5).

Figure 6-5. *The scoreManager script as a component*

If you enter the Play mode, not much will change when you kill enemies. This is because enemies have not been said to do anything in relation to incrementing the score yet. Open the enemy script and add the following line just after that responsible for destroying bullets that collide with the enemy:

```
scoreManager.instance.IncreaseScore(1);
```

This line will cause the enemy to access the `scoreManager` instance in the scene and call the `IncreaseScore` function, passing in a value of 1, which will increment the score by 1.

```
void OnCollisionEnter(Collision col) {
    if (col.gameObject.CompareTag(bulletTag)) {
        Destroy(col.gameObject);
        scoreManager.instance.IncreaseScore(1);
    }
}
```

Save the script, and when you enter Play mode this time, the score should be incremented by 1 each time you kill an enemy (Figure 6-6). Nothing will change if it is the enemy that collided with you.

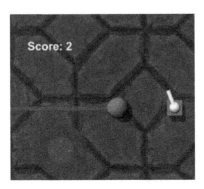

Figure 6-6. *How the score display should look like after killing two enemies*

6.3 Making Menus

In this section, we will be building three menus that the player can interact with. The first one will be displayed when the game starts, another when the player loses, and the last whenever the player pauses the game. However, we will first code everything that we will require the UI buttons of these menus to perform.

6.3.1 Coding Utilities Required

Create and open a script named utilityScript. As UI buttons can already do many things, such as disabling GameObjects, we won't have to code all the behaviors that we will require. Add the line using `UnityEngine. SceneManagement;` to the script, so that we can later call associated methods/functions.

```
public void Restart() {
  SceneManager.LoadScene(SceneManager.GetActiveScene().name);
}
```

The first function will allow the player to restart the game when they lose. Using Unity's SceneManager, we have only to load the current scene again. We do this by using the LoadScene function and passing the name of the current scene as parameter.

The next function is all about exiting the game. We use Application.Quit().

```
public void Quit() {
    Application.Quit();
}
```

To pause and unpause the game, we set the Time.timeScale value to either 0 or 1. A value of 0 will make everything unable to move.

```
public void Pause() {
    Time.timeScale = 0.0f;
}
```

```
public void UnPause() {
    Time.timeScale = 1.0f;
}
```

Finally, we pause the game as it starts, so that we can choose what to do on the first menu.

```
void Start() {
    Pause();
}
```

Here is the full code:

```
using System.Collections;
using System.Collections.Generic;
using UnityEngine;
using UnityEngine.SceneManagement;

public class utilityScript : MonoBehaviour {
    void Start() {
        Pause();
    }

    public void Restart() {    SceneManager.
    LoadScene(SceneManager.GetActiveScene().name);
    }

    public void Quit() {
        Application.Quit();
    }

    public void Pause() {
        Time.timeScale = 0.0f;
    }

    public void UnPause() {
        Time.timeScale = 1.0f;
    }
}
```

Place the script on the ScriptManager GameObject itself.

6.3.2 Start Menu

This menu will be displayed whenever the scene is loaded. In Scene, disable the SpawnPoints GameObject (untick the check box to the left of its name in the Inspector while selected). We don't want enemies to be spawned before we click the Play button.

Under Canvas, create a new empty GameObject named StartMenu. Make sure it is at the bottom of the list of children of the Canvas in the hierarchy, so that it is displayed on top of all the other elements.

Make a UI Image named Background a child of StartMenu. Give it a width and height bigger than those you are using as resolution in the Game window. I'm using a 1920 × 1080 resolution, so I will assign a width of 2500 and a height of 1250. Give the UI Image component a color of your choice and reduce its opacity a bit, if you want. I'm using a somewhat cyan color and an opacity of 190 (Figure 6-7).

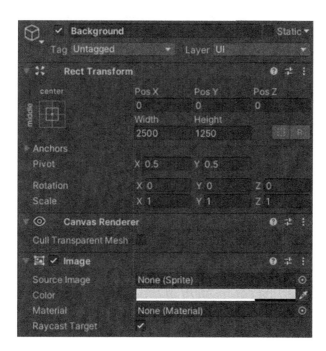

Figure 6-7. *The Background UI element*

Next, you can make a Text UI element as a child of StartMenu (Figure 6-8). Name it Title. It will be used as a label for the name of our game. Make it as big as you want, using Best Fit and align it in the center for both axes (Figure 6-9).

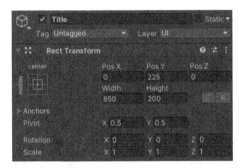

Figure 6-8. *The Rect Transform component of the Title UI element*

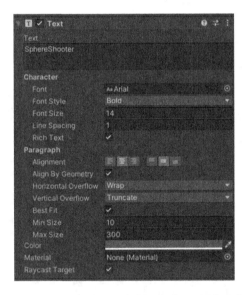

Figure 6-9. *The Text component of the Title UI element*

We only need two buttons now. Create a UI button element, still as a child of StartMenu, and name it PlayButton. I've selected a green color for the Image component of my PlayButton and made it 400 units wide, 100 units tall, and placed it at (0, -180, 0) (Figure 6-10).

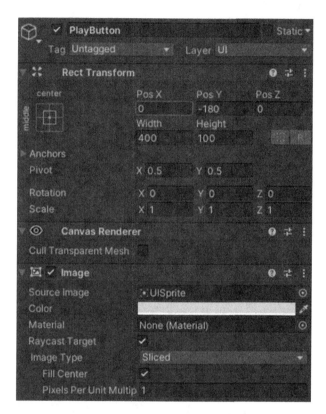

Figure 6-10. *The PlayButton UI element*

In the OnClick() part of the Button component of PlayButton (Figure 6-11), click the plus icon (+) three times. In the first slot, drag and drop in the StartMenu and select the GameObject.SetActive(bool) function, while making sure that the check box that will appear remains unchecked. In the second, do a similar thing, except using the SpawnPoints GameObject this time and making sure the check box is checked. Last, drag in the ScriptManager and choose utilityScript.UnPause().

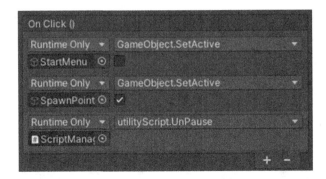

Figure 6-11. *The* OnClick *function of the Button component of*
PlayButton

To complete the PlayButton element, select its child (named Text),
make it display Play, and, optionally, change its color. Make it use a Bold
font style and tick Best Fit (Figure 6-12).

Figure 6-12. *The Text component of the child of PlayButton*

We only require the Exit button now. Duplicate PlayButton, name the new element ExitButton, give it a red color, place it at (0, -315, 0), and give its Text UI element child a value of Exit (Figure 6-13).

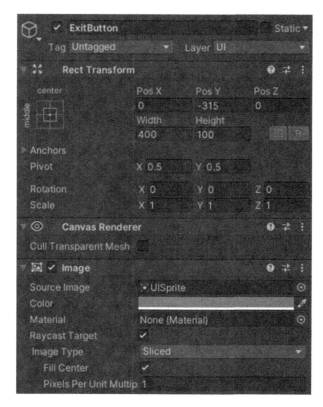

Figure 6-13.   *The Text component of the child of ExitButton*

In the OnClick() of ExitButton, reference ScriptManager and call the utilityScript.Quit() function (Figure 6-14).

Figure 6-14. *The* OnClick() *function of the Button component of* *ExitButton*

Your hierarchy should contain the following elements and GameObjects as children of the Canvas GameObject (Figure 6-15):

Figure 6-15. *The GameObjects that currently form part of the children in Canvas*

Note that clicking the Exit button in the Editor won't do anything. You can enter Play mode and make sure that the buttons work now (Figure 6-16).

Figure 6-16. *How the StartMenu looks*

6.3.3 Pause Menu

Before we make the actual Pause menu, let's make a pause button that we can press in-game. Disable the StartMenu GameObject first, so that we can preview everything we do more easily in the Game/Scene view. Download and import the following image in the Textures folder in the Project Window: `https://raw.githubusercontent.com/EdgeKing810/SphereShooter/master/Assets/Images/Pause.png`. Select it and mark it as a Sprite2D in the Inspector and hit apply (Figure 6-17).

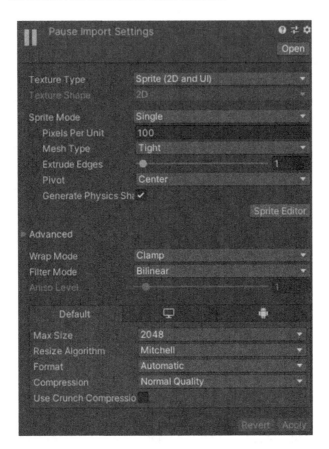

Figure 6-17. *Importing the texture of PauseButton*

Next, create a UI Button element as a child of the Canvas GameObject and place it above the StartMenu GameObject or at the top of all the children. Name it PauseButton. Duplicate the StartMenu GameObject too, name the new instance PauseMenu, and enable its GameObject (Figure 6-18).

Figure 6-18. *The GameObjects that currently form part of the children in Canvas*

Delete the Text UI element that is a child of PauseButton. You might not be able to spot the PauseButton unless you disable the GameObject of StartMenu and PauseMenu. Place PauseButton at (0, 400, 0) and make it have both a width and height of 100. In its Image component, make sure it uses the Pause Sprite as Source Image (Figure 6-19).

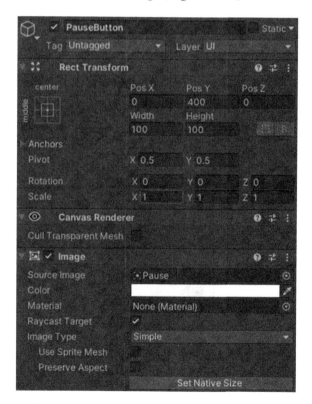

Figure 6-19. *The Rect and Image components of PauseButton*

213

The OnClick function of its Button Component should disable its own GameObject, enable that of the actual PauseMenu, and call the Pause function from the utilityScript on ScriptManager (Figure 6-20).

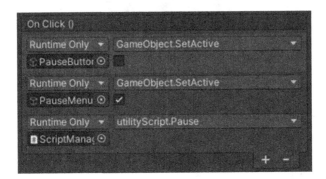

Figure 6-20. *The* OnClick *function of the Button component of PauseButton*

If you disabled the PauseMenu GameObject, re-enable it now while keeping StartMenu disabled. The Background of PauseMenu can be changed to another color, if you wish. Next, change the Title to Paused and delete the ExitButton GameObject. Rename PlayButton ResumeButton, give it a blue color, and the text Resume inside. Maybe move it a little more toward the bottom too (Figure 6-21).

Figure 6-21. *The GameObjects that currently form part of the children in Canvas*

The OnClick of ResumeButton should enable the GameObject of PauseButton, disable that of PauseMenu, and call the UnPause function from utilityScript found on ScriptManager (Figure 6-22).

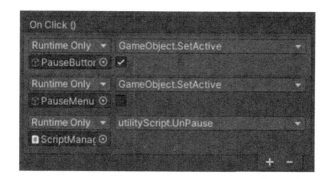

Figure 6-22. *The OnClick function of the Button component of ResumeButton*

The last thing to do is to disable the PauseMenu GameObject in the scene and enable that of StartMenu. We had done the opposite just to be able to preview how it would look. Here's what my PauseMenu looks like when I click the PauseButton while playing (Figure 6-23):

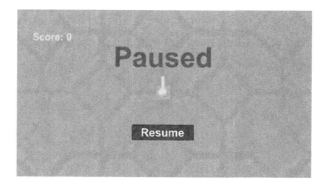

Figure 6-23. *How the PauseMenu looks*

6.3.4 Game Over Menu

You should already have guessed the use of this menu just by the name. Duplicate StartMenu, name the new instance GameOverMenu, and disable the GameObjects of both StartMenu and PauseMenu. Change the color of the Image component of the Background GameObject, display Game Over in the text of Title instead, and delete PlayButton. Rename ExitButton RestartButton, change its color, and name its Text child display Restart. Finally, make it call the Restart function of utilityScript on ScriptManager in OnClick () (Figure 6-24).

Figure 6-24. *The OnClick function of the Button component of RestartButton*

Create a new Text UI element as a child of GameOverMenu and name it ScoreLabel. Place it at (-200, -25, 0) and give it a width and height of 365 and 80, respectively. Make it display Score:, align it to the left horizontally and at the bottom vertically. Give it a Font Size of 65, mark it bold, and change its color (Figure 6-25).

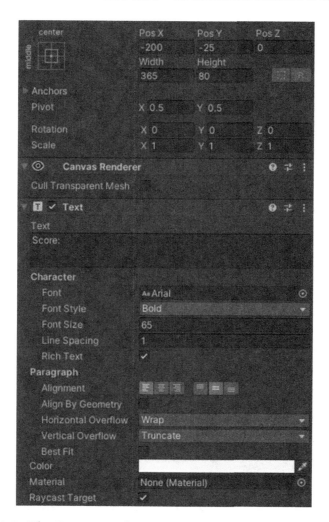

Figure 6-25. *The Rect Transform and Text components of ScoreLabel*

Duplicate that Text UI element, name it Value, and make it a child of ScoreLabel. Change its color, align it to the right horizontally, make it use a normal Font Style, and change its Rect Transform properties to have a position of (465, 0, 0) and a width and height of 250 and 80, respectively (Figure 6-26).

217

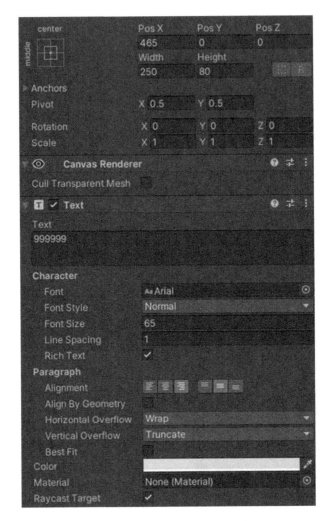

Figure 6-26. *The Rect Transform and Text components of Value*

Duplicate the ScoreLabel GameObject, rename the new instance to HighScoreLabel, make it have a position of (-200, -125, 0), change its text value to High Score:, and change its color (Figure 6-27).

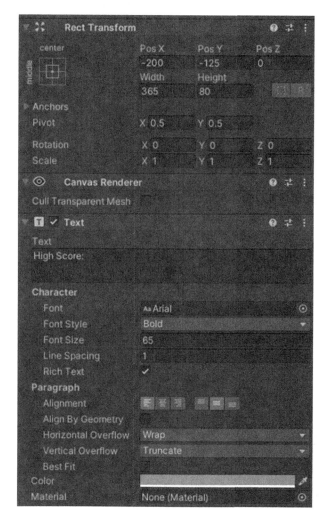

Figure 6-27. *The Rect Transform and Text components of HighScoreLabel*

My Hierarchy window looks like the following for the children of the GameOverMenu GameObject (Figure 6-28):

Figure 6-28. *The children GameObjects of GameOverMenu*

And this is what my GameOverMenu should look like later, when health mechanics are implemented, and the player loses a game (Figure 6-29):

Figure 6-29. *How the GameOverMenu looks*

Again, disable the GameObjects of PauseMenu and GameOverMenu and enable that of StartMenu.

6.4 Adding Health

We'll take a similar approach to how we implement scores for the player's health. There will be a unique script instance on the player tank with a function, so that enemies can call to decrease its health. We will also instantiate a player explosion when they lose and create what is necessary to give more context to the GameOverMenu.

First, duplicate the ScoreText UI element and name it HealthText. Change the color of the Text component, change its text to Health:, and place it at (-660, 450, 0). Make sure that the HealthText GameObject is around the same index as the one for ScoreText, so that it is not rendered below or on top of unwanted elements. Create a new script named healthManager, place it on the Player GameObject, and open it. Add the using UnityEngine.UI; line to the script, so that we are able to modify the text value of the Text elements we'll use later.

```
public static healthManager instance;
public Text healthText;

public Text scoreText;
public Text highScoreText;

int health = 5;

public GameObject explosionPrefab;
```

Again, the first variable we are creating will correspond to an instance of our script, so that it can be called from other scripts. healthText will reference the Text component of our HealthText GameObject later. As for scoreText and highScoreText, they will correspond to the Text component of the corresponding GameObjects in GameOverMenu. The integer variable health will just keep track of the amount of health the player tank currently has. It will initially have a value of 5. Last, we will be referencing an explosion prefab to be instantiated when the player dies.

221

```
void Awake() {
    if (instance) {
        Destroy(this.gameObject);
    } else {
        instance = this;
    }
    UpdateHealth();
}
```

In the Awake function of our script, we will be making sure that only one instance of it is present in the scene. Refer to section 6.2 ("Scoring") if you don't understand this snippet of code.

```
void UpdateHealth() {
    if (health <= 0) { GameOver(); return; }
    healthText.text = "Health: " + health.ToString();
}
```

In a function named UpdateHealth, we'll update the text referenced in the healthText variable to display the health of the player. If the health is less than or equal to 0, we will call a function to perform a Game Over.

```
public void ChangeHealth(int amount) {
    health += amount;
    UpdateHealth();
}
```

We will also have another function publicly accessible, so that enemies can cause damage. Of course, enemies when calling this function will pass on a negative value, such as -1.

```
void GameOver() {
    healthText.text = "Health: 0";
    Instantiate(explosionPrefab, transform.position,
    explosionPrefab.transform.rotation);
```

```
Destroy(this.gameObject);

scoreText.transform.parent.parent.gameObject.
SetActive(true);

int score = scoreManager.instance.GetCurrentScore();
scoreText.text = score.ToString();

int highScore = PlayerPrefs.GetInt("HighScore", 0);
if (score > highScore) {
    highScore = score;
    PlayerPrefs.SetInt("HighScore", highScore);
}
highScoreText.text = highScore.ToString();
}
```

In the GameOver function, we will, in short, have to destroy the player and update the score/high score text of the corresponding GameObjects in the GameOverMenu variable.

The first thing we will do is set the healthText text value to display the amount of health to be 0, spawn an explosion at the position of the player, and destroy the player tank GameObject. You should be familiar with these syntaxes.

Next, to display the actual GameOverMenu screen, we use the gameObject.SetActive method with true as parameter for the parent GameObject of the parent Transform of our scoreText Transform itself. If you look at your hierarchy, you'll see that GameOverMenu is the parent of ScoreLabel, itself the parent of Value, i.e., our scoreText. We could have referenced the GameOverMenu GameObject directly using a variable, but it is useful for you know this way of doing things.

Then, we will be creating a local integer variable named score, to which we will assign the value returned from a function we call from our scoreManager instance (which we will implement in the next steps), to get the score. We will display this in the text component referenced in the scoreText variable.

For the high score, we will first create another local variable. To this variable, we will fetch and store the previous High Score. We do this by making use of PlayerPrefs, which has the ability to store data even when the game is closed. The syntax for fetching integer data is `PlayerPrefs.GetInt(<ID>, <defaultValue>)`. In our case, the ID is HighScore. `PlayerPrefs` will search and return a stored value that is associated with that ID. If that ID doesn't exist, or no data has been saved using that ID, the default value of 0 will be returned and stored in the `highScore` variable.

We will then check whether our current score in the game we just played is greater than the High Score. If yes, we will both set the value of the `highScore` variable and the `PlayerPref` corresponding to the HighScore ID to the value of `score`. Finally, we update the value of the text component referenced in the `highScoreText` variable.

The full script follows:

```
using System.Collections;
using System.Collections.Generic;
using UnityEngine;
using UnityEngine.UI;

public class healthManager : MonoBehaviour {
    public static healthManager instance;
    public Text healthText;

    public Text scoreText;
    public Text highScoreText;

    int health = 5;

    public GameObject explosionPrefab;

    void Awake() {
        if (instance) {
            Destroy(this.gameObject);
        } else {
```

```
        instance = this;
    }
    UpdateHealth();
}

public void ChangeHealth(int amount) {
    health += amount;
    UpdateHealth();
}

void UpdateHealth() {
    if (health <= 0) { GameOver(); return; }
    healthText.text = "Health: " + health.ToString();
}

void GameOver() {
    healthText.text = "Health: 0";
    Instantiate(explosionPrefab, transform.position,
    explosionPrefab.transform.rotation);
    Destroy(this.gameObject);

    scoreText.transform.parent.parent.gameObject.
    SetActive(true);

    int score = scoreManager.instance.GetCurrentScore();
    scoreText.text = score.ToString();

    int highScore = PlayerPrefs.GetInt("HighScore", 0);
    if (score > highScore) {
        highScore = score;
        PlayerPrefs.SetInt("HighScore", highScore);
    }
    highScoreText.text = highScore.ToString();
}
}
```

For the script to properly compile and work, we must create the
GetCurrentScore function in our scoreManager script first.

```
public int GetCurrentScore() {
  return score;
}
```

That function can be publicly called and will return an integer value ;
that is held in the score variable.

Save both of the scripts. Back in the Editor, assign the corresponding
components to the fields of healthManager. Don't forget that this script
should be on your Player GameObject (Figure 6-30).

Figure 6-30. *The healthManager script as a component*

Health Text will correspond to the Text component of the HealthText
GameObject you created at the start of this section. Score Text and High
Score Text will then correspond to the Text component of the GameObject
named Value that is the child of the ScoreLabel and HighScoreLabel
GameObjects, respectively. As the Explosion Prefab, I am using the FX_
Explosion_Rubble prefab from SimpleFX ➤ Prefabs.

Additionally, we have to modify the enemy script, so that enemies can
cause damage. Edit the OnCollisionEnter function, to verify if the object
that collided is the player and, if that is the case, call the ChangeHealth
function on the healthManager instance.

226

```
if (col.gameObject.CompareTag(playerTag))  {
    healthManager.instance.ChangeHealth(-1);
}
```

I've also gone ahead and modified the OnCollisionEnter function, so that there is a little less code duplication and the overall look is cleaner. You don't need to do that, though.

```
void OnCollisionEnter(Collision col) {
    if (col.gameObject.CompareTag(bulletTag))  {
        Destroy(col.gameObject);
        scoreManager.instance.IncreaseScore(1);
        DestroyEnemy();
    }

    if (col.gameObject.CompareTag(playerTag))  {
        healthManager.instance.ChangeHealth(-1);
        DestroyEnemy();
    }
}
```

Now, if you play the game, you will see that the HealthText text gets updated when enemies collide with you. When your health reaches 0, an explosion will be seen along with the GameOverMenu, which will be displayed with the correct score and highScore values.

You will also notice errors when you lose (Figure 6-31).

Figure 6-31. *Errors being caused from the cameraFollow script*

These have to do with the cameraFollow script not being able to follow the player tank when it is destroyed, because it corresponds to a value of null. Edit the cameraFollow script and add a check to prevent that error from occurring when the player tank is destroyed and, thus, doesn't exist.

```
void LateUpdate() {
  if (player) {
    this.transform.position = new Vector3(player.position.x,
height, player.position.z);
  }
}
```

6.5 A New Enemy

While the current enemy does its job quite well, let's introduce a new enemy that takes three shots to be destroyed. It will also cause more damage if it collides with the player.

Start by duplicating the Enemy prefab in the Project window. Name the new instance EnemyBig and the original one EnemySmall. Double-click to open the EnemyBig prefab (Figure 6-32). Give it a Scale of (3, 3, 3), and change its color and that of its Trail Renderer child by making use of a new material. I'll also be making the Trail Renderer wider by using a width of 0.75. Finally, we will also want to reduce the Max Speed value of the enemy script on the EnemyBig GameObject to something like 3 and use another explosion prefab. For this, I will be using the SimpleFX ➤ Prefabs ➤ FX_Fireworks_Blue_Large, but with an orange color.

Figure 6-32. *The components on the new Enemy GameObject*

Let's now modify the script responsible for spawning enemies, enemySpawner, so that it randomly spawns either of our two enemies prefabs. The first thing we have to do is transform the `public GameObject` enemy statement to one that refers to an array of GameObjects with the identifier "enemies": `public GameObject[] enemies`.

Then, add a line of code before the line containing the instantiate instruction, to create a local GameObject variable, named enemy, that will be assigned a random (enemy) GameObject from the enemies array.

```
void SpawnEnemy() {
    int randomPos = (int)Random.Range(0, transform.childCount);
    GameObject enemy = enemies[(int)Random.Range(0, enemies.
    Length)];
```

```
Instantiate(enemy, transform.GetChild(randomPos).position,
enemy.transform.rotation);
}
```

Back in the Editor, drag the two enemy prefabs in their corresponding slots of the enemySpawner component found on the SpawnPoints GameObject (Figure 6-33).

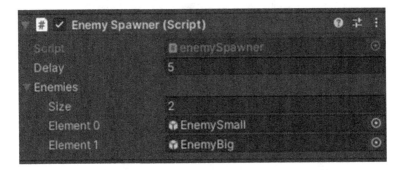

Figure 6-33. *The updated enemySpawner script as a component*

You should now be able to see the new enemy getting instantiated when you play, but it is still behaving like the original one. Open the enemy script. Time to make some changes.

We'll be using two new variables: `health` and `damageToCause`. Both will be global integer-type variables and publicly accessible, with a default value of 1.

```
public int health = 1;
public int damageToCause = 1;
```

Save the script, then, on the EnemyBig Prefab in the Project window, set both of these variables to have a value of 3 (Figure 6-34).

Figure 6-34. *The final properties of components of the EnemyBig GameObject*

Then, modify the OnCollisionEnter function so that when an enemy collides with a bullet, this reduces its health by one (health--), instead of calling the DestroyEnemy function. If an enemy collides with the player, it should cause an amount of damage equal to the value held in the damageToCause variable, so just replace the -1 value that was being passed to the ChangeHealth function of the healthManager script instance to -damageToCause. Finally, add a check, so that the DestroyEnemy function is called if the health of an enemy is less or equal to 0.

```
void OnCollisionEnter(Collision col) {
    if (col.gameObject.CompareTag(bulletTag))  {
        Destroy(col.gameObject);
```

```
        scoreManager.instance.IncreaseScore(1);
        health--;
    }

    if (col.gameObject.CompareTag(playerTag))  {
    healthManager.instance.ChangeHealth(-damageToCause);
        DestroyEnemy();
    }

    if (health <= 0) {
        DestroyEnemy();
    }
}
```

Save the script and head over to Play mode. You should see that EnemyBig GameObjects takes three bullet hits to be destroyed, and if they collide with the player tank, cause a damage of 3.

To complete this section, let's add something more to the enemy script, so that enemies get faster over time, to make the game less boring (not that it was, but whatever).

In the first line of the Start function of the enemy script, in addition to the speed variable, add the value of (Time.time / 25). The first method we're calling will return the amount of seconds, because the game started, and we are, in short, making sure that the speed of enemies being spawned will increase by 1 every 25 seconds.

```
void Start() {
 speed = Random.Range(minSpeed, maxSpeed) + (Time.time / 25);
 audioSource = GetComponent<AudioSource>();
 player = GameObject.FindWithTag(playerTag);
}
```

6.6 HealthBoxes

This is the last section in which we will be making modifications to the game. I will introduce a little cube that will be spawned randomly along the area of the Ground GameObject at defined intervals. If the player tank collides with one of these little cubes, which we will refer to as healthBoxes, we will increase their health by a certain value.

6.6.1 Making the healthBox

In your scene, create a 3D Object ➤ Cube GameObject. Name it healthBox and give it a position of (0, 1, 3), a rotation of (0, 0, 0), and a scale of (0.4, 0.4, 0.4). You can also assign a material of a green color to it. Then, check the isTrigger property of its Box Collider component (Figure 6-35).

Figure 6-35. *The components on the healthBox GameObject*

As we made the healthBox GameObject have an isTrigger collider, enemies can go right through it without requiring us to mess with the Tags and Layers properties. Our player tank can also just pick it up and continue its route unaffected from the direction we want it to go, because no collisions are occurring.

6.6.2 Adding Health

Right now, if you play, the player tank just goes through the healthBox GameObject, and there's really nothing more that happens. To make the tank interactable and give it a meaning in the game, we must code a script that defines what should happen. Create a script, name it healthBox, and open it.

We will require a function to run when an isTrigger collision occurs, and if it was the player tank's collider that was the cause of this, we must call the function to increase the player's health and destroy the GameObject of the healthBox. If we didn't perform this last step, the player could continuously move on and off the same healthBox to increase their life. We will also increase the health of the player by 2, but you can choose another value.

The full script is given following. Save it, and place it on the healthBox GameObject in the scene. You will also notice that we are using the OnTriggerEnter function with a Collider type reference passed as parameter. The function will be performed in a similar way to the famous OnCollisionEnter function we have been using all along, but this time, for treating trigger collisions.

```
using System.Collections;
using System.Collections.Generic;
using UnityEngine;
```

```
public class healthBox : MonoBehaviour {
   void OnTriggerEnter(Collider col) {
       if (col.gameObject.CompareTag("Player")) {
           healthManager.instance.ChangeHealth(2);
           Destroy(this.gameObject);
       }
   }
}
```

When you enter the Play mode now, you should notice that the healthBox GameObject gets destroyed, and your health increases by 2 (or the value you have selected in the previous step) when you "collide" with it.

6.6.3 Spawning healthBoxes Along the Map

Turn the healthBox GameObject in a prefab and delete it from your scene (Figure 6-36).

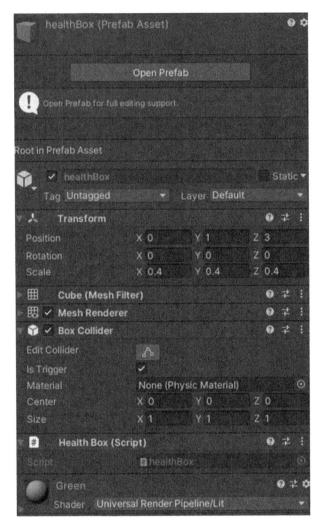

Figure 6-36. *The healthBox GameObject after being turned in a prefab*

Create another script, name it healthBoxSpawner, and open it. We will be using three variables that will be used to, respectively, reference the GameObject of the healthBox prefab, the Transform of the Ground GameObject in our scene, and hold a value that will define at what intervals to spawn a healthBox GameObject, in a similar way to the enemySpawner script.

```
public GameObject healthBox;
public Transform ground;
public float delay = 3.0f;
```

As in the case of the Start function in the enemySpawner script, we must call a function every x seconds, as defined in the delay variable to instantiate a healthBox GameObject.

```
void Start() {
    InvokeRepeating("SpawnHealthBox", 0.0f, delay);
}
```

As our Ground GameObject has a scale of magnitude 150 along its x and z axes, and the origin (0, 0, 0) is at its center, any GameObject to be at its edge must have an x and/or z position of 75 or -75. So, we will pick a random value between 75 and -75 for both the x and y value at which we want to instantiate a healthBox in the SpawnHealthBox function.

For example, to get a random value for the position along the x axis, we would use the following code:

```
float xPos = Random.Range(-1.0f, 1.0f) * (ground.localScale.x / 2);
```

Scale is always expressed locally for GameObjects. The ground.localScale.x value divided by 2 will give us 75, and we just multiply that by a random value between -1 and 1.

We will do the same to get a value for the z axis. The y axis value will be 1. Then, it is just about creating a Vector3 variable and instantiating a healthBox at that position. Quaternion.identity can be interpreted as 0 rotation along all axes.

```
void SpawnHealthBox() {
    float xPos = Random.Range(-1.0f, 1.0f) * (ground.
    localScale.x / 2);
    float zPos = Random.Range(-1.0f, 1.0f) * (ground.
    localScale.z / 2);
```

```
    Vector3 spawnPos = new Vector3(xPos, 1, zPos);

    Instantiate(healthBox, spawnPos, Quaternion.identity);
}
```

Here's the full script, in case you missed something. Save it and drag it on the SpawnPoints GameObject in your scene, because we want it to run only when we are playing the game (not before the player clicks Play, pauses the game, or loses).

```
using System.Collections;
using System.Collections.Generic;
using UnityEngine;

public class healthBoxSpawner : MonoBehaviour {

    public GameObject healthBox;
    public Transform ground;
    public float delay = 3.0f;

    void Start() {
        InvokeRepeating("SpawnHealthBox", 0.0f, delay);
    }

    void SpawnHealthBox() {
        float xPos = Random.Range(-1.0f, 1.0f) * (ground.
        localScale.x / 2);
        float zPos = Random.Range(-1.0f, 1.0f) * (ground.
        localScale.z / 2);

        Vector3 spawnPos = new Vector3(xPos, 1, zPos);

        Instantiate(healthBox, spawnPos, Quaternion.identity);
    }
}
```

Drag and drop the healthBox prefab in the Health Box field and the Ground GameObject in the Ground field. You can set another value for the Delay instead of 3 (Figure 6-37).

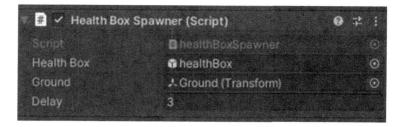

Figure 6-37. *The healthBoxSpawner script as a component*

6.7 Exporting the Game as an .apk file

We now have a fully functional game! Let's make an .apk file, so that we can install it on our Android phones and show off to our friends!

If you followed along with this book, from the point at which we downloaded a version of the Unity Editor from the Hub and installed Android modules to it, your Edit ➤ Preferences ➤ External Tools tab should look like this (Figure 6-38):

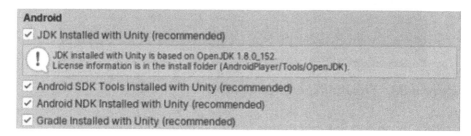

Figure 6-38. *Tools for building for the Android Platform*

Save your scene and project. Enter the Build Settings window (File ➤ Build Settings, or Ctrl+Shift+B). The first thing to do is add all the scenes you want to be present in your .apk (Figure 6-39). We have only one scene, so click Add Open Scenes. If we had multiple scenes, we'd drag them all in, the first one being the one we want the player to see when the game is opened (Figure 6-39).

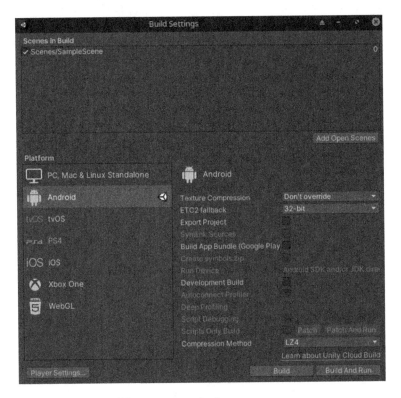

Figure 6-39. *The Build Settings window*

Click the Player Settings button at the bottom-left corner of that window. We will modify some settings first, before hitting Build. The Project Settings window will come up, and you'll be on the Player tab. The Player is the place from which we customize various options for the final game built by Unity. We will only be looking at the most frequently used options for building an Android game. The first thing that we can do is set a company name (your name as a developer, maybe), a product name (the name of our game), and set a version number (such as 1, 2, 3.5, etc.). These can be set to anything you want.

You already know how to import textures from the step in which we imported one for the Pause button (section 6.3.3, "Pause Menu"). We can then assign an icon and a cursor to our game. By default, if left empty, the icon will be that of Unity's logo, and the cursor will be blank (Figure 6-40).

Figure 6-40. *The first options in the Player tab*

I won't be covering the settings under Icon, but, in brief, you can specify textures of various resolutions to match the final icon size on various phones. It will scale the image we added in the Default Icon property accordingly, if not tweaked anyway, so it is not something you absolutely must do.

Under Resolution and Presentation (Figure 6-41), you can personalize how you want your game to be presented on phones. The options are pretty self-explanatory and easy to understand. We won't be changing anything in this section, except that we want our game to play only in a landscape mode. We can keep the Default Resolution set to Auto Rotation but unselect the Portrait modes below, or just choose another option instead of the Auto Rotation one. You can also get an idea of what many settings do, by keeping your mouse cursor hovered over one for a few seconds.

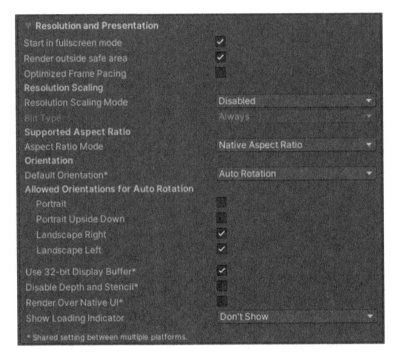

Figure 6-41. *Resolution and Presentation in the Player Settings*

Under the Splash Image tab (Figure 6-42), you can choose to display something when a user enters your game, such as the cover image of your game developer company and such. You can't set it to not display the Made by Unity logo in the Personal edition. You can set the Splash Style or Animation, or even set a background (rather than a solid color), to customize your splash screen.

If you want to display other images, add them in the Logos list, along with the amount of time you want them to be present on the screen.

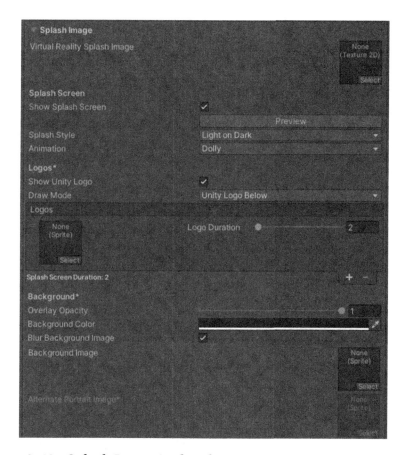

Figure 6-42. *Splash Image in the Player Settings*

Under Other Settings, we first have some settings about rendering and graphics that we don't really have to mess with (Figure 6-43). We also have the package name of our game that will be the full identifier of our game on our phone. No games or apps should have the same package name. While the version serves to identify releases of your game to you, every update that you make to your game should have a higher Bundle Version Code number than the previous one for your Android phone, to not throw errors and install it. The Minimum and Target API Levels serve to represent the range of Android phone versions that your game can be installed on.

If you try to install the .apk on an Android phone with an Android version not falling in this range, it will fail.

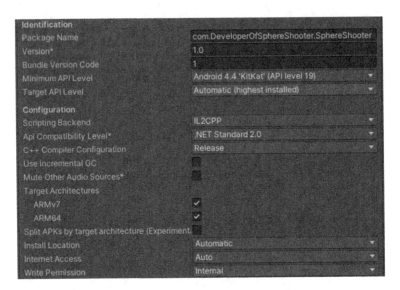

Figure 6-43. *Identification and configuration in Other Settings*

As for the Configuration part, you have to switch to the IL2CPP Scripting Backend, to target devices with an ARM64 architecture (under Target Architectures; see Figure 6-43) and if you want your game to be accepted later (if you submit it) to Google's Play Store. Our game will already be pretty performant; there is no need to tweak any other options.

Finally, we can make a Keystore and "sign" our game, so that it has the identity of the person who made it. Phones and the Play Store will also deny updates to a game/app if signed with a key that is not the one that was used for the first version submitted.

Click the Keystore Manager button, create a new keystone, fill in the details, and click the Add Key button (Figure 6-44).

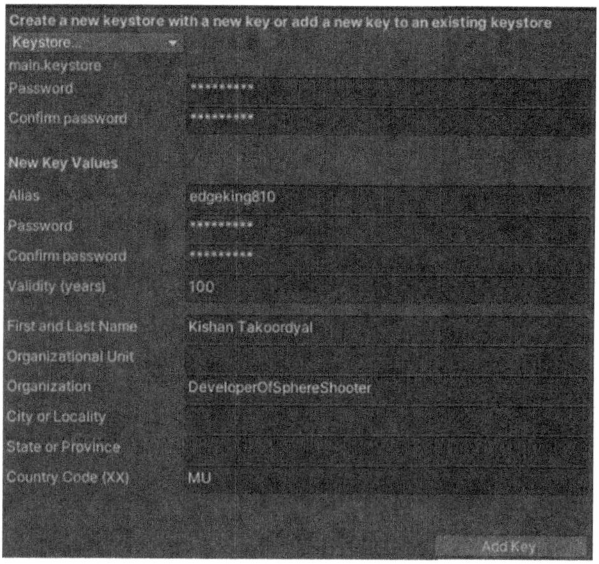

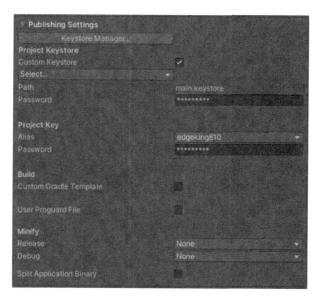

Figure 6-44. *The Keystore Manager window*

Then, input the same details in the Publishing Settings section of the Player (Figure 6-45).

Figure 6-45. *Publishing Settings in the Player*

If later on you make games that after being built have .apk files that occupy more than 100MB, you must tick Split Application Binary, which that will create an additional expansion file (OBB file) and reduce the size of the .apk file, so that Google Play accepts it.

Finally, click Build in the Build Settings window and specify the location and name of the .apk file that is going to be generated (Figure 6-46). Then, just wait. If the build fails, check your Console window for errors and simply Google them.

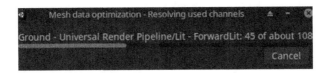

Figure 6-46. *One of the processes that runs when we click Build*

One common error on Windows has to do with licenses of the Android SDK modules not having been accepted. To fix this, you must go to the location where the Android SDK has been downloaded/installed and execute the following command in a CMD window. Replace the Unity Editor version with your own.

```
cd "Program Files\Unity\Hub\Editor\2019.3.0b12\Editor\Data\
PlaybackEngines\AndroidPlayer\SDK\tools\bin"
```

```
sdkmanager.bat --licenses
```

If you get any other errors, just search and try to find a solution. If you still are not able to get your game to build properly, download and install the Android SDK, NDK, JDK, and Gradle manually and point Unity to their location in the Edit ➤ Preferences window.

Note   Following is what my External Tools tab looks like on Linux (Figure 6-47). I wasn't getting it to work with the included Android tools I had downloaded along Unity in the Hub, so I manually unpacked/installed all of them, and now my game builds properly. If you proceed to this step, you can follow along not-too-dated forum posts and find articles easily. Note that for some tools, such as JDK and NDK, Unity supports very specific versions.

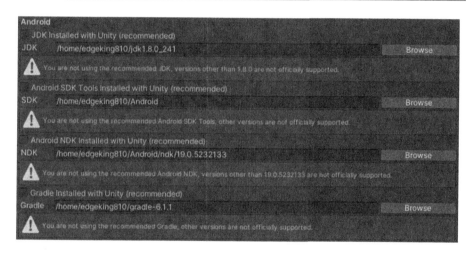

Figure 6-47. *My External Tools window*

Once you have your .apk file, send it to your phone. and in a file manager app on your phone, just browse to where the .apk file is and install it (Figure 6-48). You can now play the game you made and show it to your friends!

Figure 6-48. *The final .apk file*

There are still many things that can be done in Sphere Shooter if you want to build your skills and make a better game. Here's a short list:

- Add more sound effects and Particle Systems.

- Implement a feature that allows the player to choose from a couple of looks for the Ground GameObject's textures.

- Add more enemies: one that is smaller and faster, one that spawns smaller enemies when killed, one that can stick to the player and reduce their max speed.

- Add coins to the game that allow the player to buy more turrets for their tank.

- Increase the value of a kill the longer the player survives.

- Add more tanks with lasers, projectiles, and flamethrowers.

- Implement something like Challenges in the game, with rewards upon completion.

You can also refer to a game named Balls and Turrets, which at its core is Sphere Shooter. Find it on Google Play.

I hope you enjoyed this book as much as I did writing it! We looked at several concepts of game development and how to use many of the features that Unity offers. We even made a demo game that can be heavily improved and built on. I am glad if you have considered a career in game development after having read this book. Please don't hesitate to learn more on the topic and build great and fun games. Share them with me. I'd love to see your creations.

Index

© Kishan Takoordyal 2020
K. Takoordyal, *Beginning Unity Android Game Development*,
https://doi.org/10.1007/978-1-4842-6002-9

Printed in the United States
By Bookmasters